Jessica's Raw Chocolate Recipes

Jessica's Raw Chocolate Recipes

natural
power food
for the
chocoholic

Jessica Fenton

Leaping Hare Press

First published in the UK in 2011 by

Leaping Hare Press

210 High Street, Lewes
East Sussex BN7 2NS, UK
www.leapingharepress.co.uk

British Library Cataloguing-in-Publication Data
A catalogue record for this book is available from the British Library

ISBN: 978-1-907332-71-5

This book was conceived, designed and produced by

Leaping Hare Press

Creative Director: Peter Bridgewater
Publisher: Jason Hook
Commissioning Editor: Monica Perdoni
Editorial Director: Tom Kitch
Senior Designer: James Lawrence
Designer: JC Lanaway
Recipe photography: Clive Streeter
Food stylist: Teresa Goldfinch
Location photography: Rob Streeter
Hair and make-up stylist: Dee Howland

Printed in China
Colour Origination by Ivy Press Reprographics

10 9 8 7 6 5 4 3 2 1

Contents

Author's Introduction   6

Part 1: Raw Chocolate – from Bean to Butter 8

Raw Chocolate – a History   10
Health Benefits   12
A Guide to Ingredients   14
Making the Most of Raw Chocolate   18
Raw Chocolate Equipment   20
Basic Recipes   22

Part 2: The Recipes 24

Drinks

Raw Chocochino/Cacao & Coconut Water Shake   26
Cacao Maca Boost/Choctail Mocktail   28
Raw Chocolate & Banana Smoothie/
  Winter Warming Drinking Chocolate   30

Sweets

Raw Chocolate-coated Brazils	32
Raw Cacao Fudge	34
Tangy Lemon Chocolates	36
Fresh Cherry & Chocolate Truffles	38
White & Dark Orange Creams	40
Double-dunked Raw Chocolate Truffles	42
Cinnamon-flavoured Raw Chocolate Bars	44
Peppermint Creams	46
Ginger Caramels	48
Almond Butter Truffles	50

Biscuits & Cakes

Raw Chocolate Cheesecake	52
Raw Chocolate Brownies	54
Rich Raw Chocolate & Vanilla Torte	56
Chocolate Goji Finger Biscuits	58
White Chocolate & Raisin Snaps	60
Raw Chocolate Gingerbread People	62
Love Macaroons	64

Desserts

Neapolitan Ice Cream	66
Summer Sorbet/Beetroot & Mint Choc Chip Sorbet	68
Guarana & Goji Nutty Loaf	70
Little Leo's Pudding	72
White Raw Choc Chip Pudding	74
Tingly Raw Chocolate Body Paint	76

Party Food

Raw Hemp & Chocolate Spread	78
Raw Chocolate Jellies	80
Crêpes	82
Banana Split	84
Birthday Cake	86
Ice Cream Sandwich	88
Raw Ice Cream Sundae	90
Milk Chocolate Fruit & Nut Clusters	92
Cacao Crackers with Spicy Tomato & Cacao Salad Cream	94

Index	96

My Lifelong Love of Chocolate

I think it's fair to say that I've been mesmerized by chocolate right from the earliest age. I can't put my finger on exactly what it is about the magical brown stuff that reels me in so deeply, almost in a hypnotic way. In fact, even the sound of the word 'chocolate' never fails to make my face light up and in more recent years evokes through my senses a nostalgic state of mind.

There's something so special about chocolate, it's no wonder that it effortlessly maintains its luxurious, decadent profile. But what's remarkable is that having started at such a tender age, my relationship with chocolate has since grown healthier by the day.

How I Got into Raw Foods

It's my health-pioneering mother who I have to thank for the journey I embarked on as a young adult to find, research and then reveal the ultimate truth behind nutrition and the fundamental part it plays in achieving long-term optimum health.

We were the only children at our school to eat organic food. No one around us seemed to know what it was back then in the 1980s, as it was years before the organic food revolution really hit. Teachers and dinner ladies alike would try an organic crisp from our biodegradable bag with a mixture of interest and caution. My mum and dad were not overly well off when we were growing up, but would nevertheless set aside a large part of their household budget to allow for a weekly organic food delivery. Suzanne would appear without fail each week, come rain, snow or shine, and unpack crates of overpriced, organic versions of popular mainstream foods from her white van. Organic food was proportionately much more expensive than non-organic at that time, even more so than it is today, simply because there was much less demand for it then.

When I was sixteen, I was diagnosed with glandular fever and within three years I had developed Myalgic

Encephalomyelitis (ME)/Chronic Fatigue Syndrome (CFS). Little did I know in my bedridden state that this was the start of my career in natural nutrition. I adopted a vegan diet free of refined sugars, wheat and gluten and then went on to eat a diet abundant in plant-based whole foods in their glorious, natural, raw, 'enzymatic' state. I successfully ridded my body of CFS, at the same time as adding years of vitality to the rest of my life. I went on to run the London Marathon in a little over four hours, in celebration of the fact that I simply could.

Raw Versus Roasted

The chocolate recipes I present in this book differ from those in nearly every other chocolate recipe book on the market in one major respect – they feature raw chocolate only. So what actually is raw chocolate? As the term suggests, it's basically chocolate made from unroasted ingredients. Cacao (pronounced *cac-cow*) originates from the seed of the cacao pod that is fermented like conventional cocoa but has not gone on to be roasted or heat treated above 45°C/113°F. When cacao remains in its unroasted state, it retains a large proportion of its nutrients, antioxidants and phytochemicals. In other words, it offers a wide spectrum of health benefits for you and your family to enjoy.

Raw Chocolate – A Healthy Luxury for Everyone

We can all benefit from eating raw chocolate in place of roasted chocolate regardless of what other foods and drinks we consume in our daily diet, because this type of chocolate is truly a luxurious, wellbeing-enhancing gift from Mother Nature. But if you are looking to achieve improved health and greater energy levels, you can also make a conscious effort to include other plant-based foods in their natural state in your daily diet.

Dedication

For my soul mate: Tom BF Fenton, and our beloved son, Leo Finley. Thank you for such an exciting adventure. Also, huge appreciation to the rest of my family and close friends. Thanks to all those who support me in my ultimate mission of making raw food famous. In particular my adorable mum, who's a superb babysitter!

Raw Chocolate
– From Bean to Butter

Raw Chocolate – a History

Chocolate isn't just a modern-day ingredient found in confectionery bars, it has been an essential food throughout the ages. Its long, rich history dates back to around 2000 BCE, before the ancient Olmec civilization, and cacao-bean mixtures were the beverages of choice of the Aztec, Mayans and Incas. Cacao beans were historically used as money as well as an aphrodisiac ingredient.

It was the Spanish explorer Hernando Cortés who introduced cacao beans to Europe in 1519, after having been presented with them when he arrived in Mexico by the Aztecs, who believed him to be their long-awaited god. From chocolate's first introduction into Spain the fascination with chocolate continued to spread throughout Europe, although the treasured cacao beans themselves were kept a secret for a further one hundred years.

The first chocolate house opened in London in 1657, and proved to be a favourite meeting place for the elite and wealthy. Nearly a hundred years later, the Swedish naturalist scientist Carolus Linnaeus renamed the European word 'cocoa' to Theobroma cacao, which is Greek for 'food of the gods'.

It wasn't until the early 1990s that the health benefits associated with cacao started to reach the public consciousness and its popularity in this regard began to grow. Instrumental in this was the introduction of the first organic chocolate bar, followed soon after by an organic Fair Trade chocolate bar. Raw cacao beans were on sale on a small scale in places like Glastonbury and Brighton, but they remained in relative obscurity.

American raw food advocate David Wolfe took a sample of his Ecuadorian raw chocolate powder along to the US Department of Agriculture (USDA) at Brunswick Laboratories, Massachusetts. Here it was revealed that there were 955 ORAC (Oxygen Radical Absorbance Capacity) units in a single gram of raw cacao powder, compared to just 260 in regular dark cocoa powder – ORAC units being the USDA's measure of antioxidant capacity (see page 12). It was from this point onwards that the real raw chocolate breakthrough began to emerge.

Raw Cacao Powder

Green is the New Black

The process used to achieve premium-quality raw cacao products differs from the way that regular cocoa is commercially processed. Raw cacao farming and processing is more environmentally sound, because it's a far less energy-intensive procedure from start to finish. Raw cacao usually comes from small-scale growers who do not employ children or pay their workers a low wage. In fact, most operate in quite the opposite manner, under Fair Trade schemes where the workers are paid and treated fairly in return for their high-quality crops. This ethos is further extended in some cases where eco companies have formed to work closely with local communities, offering their workers a better standard of living by providing accommodation, food, financial advice and farming support. The farmers tend to use growing and processing methods that are of traditional origin (for example, sun drying and stone milling), and many farms are naturally free from agricultural chemicals or pesticides, with some now being organically certified.

The raw chocolate-making process

- The raw cacao beans are collected from the pods.
- The cacao beans are then cleaned to remove all extraneous material.
- The fermentation process takes 2–3 days and the temperatures are kept low (40–45°C/104–113°F).
- They are then dried and top-grade beans are selected for their size and shape.
- The raw cacao beans are heated to 40°C/104°F so that they can be peeled and broken into nibs.
- The nibs are cold pressed into a cake to release the oil that separates the fibre and protein. This is the most difficult part of the process to keep raw, as it's often done by a hydraulic press where the temperature can reach 80°C/176°F for a few seconds if it isn't correctly monitored. This process separates the oil from the cake, which is collected separately and goes on to form the raw cacao butter.
- The cake is then cold ground and sifted to remove the larger particles. This then forms raw cacao powder.

Health Benefits

Numerous scientific research studies have shown that cacao is good for your health, with new studies being carried out and findings published all the time. But it's my view that there are even more powerful medicinal and health benefits in relation to raw chocolate yet to be revealed, as this is just the start of the unveiling of the best-kept secret in the health industry.

Essential Nutrients

It's now being reported that raw cacao, largely due to the fact that it remains in its raw state, contains roughly a third more essential nutrients than roasted cocoa.

Magnesium – the Heart Mineral

Raw chocolate is one of the highest food sources of magnesium. Magnesium is involved in healthy heart function, energy production, nerve function, muscle relaxation and bone and tooth formation. It also balances brain chemistry and decreases blood coagulation, which can result in the reduction of a person's overall blood pressure. It has been estimated that 68 per cent of Americans are magnesium deficient, although I concur with the many others in this nutritional field who estimate that the figure has risen closer to 80 per cent.

Sulphur – the Beauty Mineral

Another reason to eat raw cacao is that it contains high levels of the beauty mineral sulphur. Sulphur is involved in liver detoxification and for building strong hair, nails and skin.

Antioxidants

Raw cacao is proven to be roughly seven times higher in antioxidants than standard plain chocolate, making it the richest source of antioxidants, according to the ORAC Unit rating scale developed by the USDA (*see* page 10). Antioxidants are substances that help maintain a youthful appearance by inhibiting the oxidation of cell membranes. The body's cells are protected from the oxidative damage that free radicals can cause by literally mopping up these harmful molecules. What's more, because the raw chocolate recipes in this book exclude the use of dairy products, the powerful antioxidant flavonols are not blocked in any way during absorption.

The Uplifting Effects of Raw Cacao

Raw chocolate contains phenylethylamine (PEA), which is a naturally occurring chemical that is also released from our brain in larger quantities when we are in love (however, currently it's not known how much PEA from raw chocolate reaches the brain). Other exciting properties of raw cacao include the natural phytochemical anandamide, also known as 'the bliss chemical', which can propel us into a blissful feeling of wellbeing. This is further intensified by the enzyme inhibitors contained within cacao, which increase the length of time that anandamide stays in circulation in the body. This may intensify the 'feel good' feelings associated with raw chocolate.

Theobromine and Caffeine

Chocolate has long been associated with the stimulating effects of caffeine, but in reality raw cacao contains only traceable amounts of caffeine – much less than you may think. Unique to cacao is an alkaloid called theobromine, which is similar to (but not the same as) caffeine, yet it has a much milder effect. In any case, raw caffeine has a lesser impact on the body when absorbed in its naturally occurring, raw state than when roasted. It's important to note, however, that theobromine can have a toxic effect when consumed by dogs and cats.

Essential Fats

Raw cacao butter contains no cholesterol, and it is rich in monounsaturated fat, which can help lower harmful low-density lipoprotein (LPL) cholesterol. The main 'mono' fat in cacao butter is oleic acid, which is also abundant in other plant-based foods and products such as olive oil and avocado. Over half the saturated fat content of raw cacao comes from stearic acid, which has a neutral effect on blood cholesterol. In moderate amounts, the fats contained in raw cacao are not harmful to the body.

Balancing Out Raw Chocolate

I feel strongly that the presence of organic green leafy vegetables in the diet is especially important when consuming raw chocolate because the chlorophyll, otherwise known as the 'blood' of the leaf, works synergistically with the cacao.

If you have consumed raw cacao and want to lessen the euphoric feeling that you might have encountered from doing so, I find eating cardamom seeds can be very helpful.

A Guide to Ingredients

The following pages detail the nutrient-dense ingredients featured in the recipes in the book, so stock up on them to make the most nutritious chocolate dishes and treats imaginable. You'll find these fantastic, natural plant-based ingredients in your local health-food shop or online, and many of them are suitable for use in other recipes too.

Raw Cacao Nibs

These are great in raw chocolate recipes as the equivalent of chocolate chips. The nibs are slightly harder than regular chocolate chips (which contain refined sugar), but are truly delicious. They can also be ground down and used in place of raw cacao powder if you run out, but bear in mind that the result will taste quite different and far less chocolatey than the cacao powder version, since cacao nibs have not had their fat extracted.

Raw Cacao Paste

I don't use raw cacao paste very much in my raw chocolate recipes because it can have rather a bitter taste and therefore requires a substantial amount of natural sweetener to stabilize the flavour. But I do like to use it in my Raw Cacao Fudge recipe (*see* page 34), where it produces a truly rich-tasting result.

Raw Cacao Powder

This is my staple raw cacao ingredient. It's light and fluffy as a powder yet becomes full bodied when blended. Raw cacao powder is often such high quality that only a few tablespoons are required to achieve a real depth of flavour.

Raw Cacao Butter

Raw Cacao Butter

An ingredient I use frequently in my recipes, cacao butter acts as a solidifier and hardens the chocolate once it has set. To speed up this process, I usually recommend placing your raw chocolate in the freezer to harden. Cacao butter has a melting temperature of just below body temperature, like conventional chocolate.

Raw Cacao Powder

The Real Deal

Don't confuse raw chocolate powder with standard cocoa, or worse still drinking chocolate, which contains refined sugar and dried milk powder. Neither of these types of chocolate contains the wide range of nutrients beneficial to your health that can be found in raw cacao.

Raw Cacao Beans

I usually reserve the use of raw cacao beans for savoury dishes, as the whole bean brings out the heat and flavour of the dish. I prefer using raw cacao beans with their skins on because they contain higher amounts of iron.

Yacon Syrup

This sweet liquid is pressed from the yacon root, a distant relative of the sunflower that has been ecologically grown and consumed in the Peruvian Andes for centuries, and was used by the Incas. It's a toffee-tasting, glucose-free, low-calorie sweetener that is thought to improve digestive health, as it contains a unique type of fructose called fructo-oligosaccharide (FOS). FOS is largely indigestible, yet feeds the friendly bacteria within the colon. Yacon can be used as a sweetener for those with a candida imbalance as well as blood sugar imbalances. It's also favoured by diabetics and people with renal and digestive disorders as a substitute for refined sugar and honey.

Lecithin Granules

These granules are rich in the two important nutrients associated with fat metabolism: inositol and choline. Lecithin is important for brain health as it's a natural source of phosphatidyl serine (PS). A person's PS levels start to reduce with age, which makes this supplement particularly beneficial in later years.

Xylitol Crystals

Xylitol (pronounced *zy-ler-tol*) is found in the fibres of many plant foods in small amounts and in larger amounts in fruits, berries, lettuce, corn on the cob and mushrooms. It can also be extracted from birch, raspberries and plums. Xylitol crystals look and taste like refined sugar granules, although they have a slight

Xylitol Crystals

cooling effect in the mouth. They can be used as a direct substitute for sugar, but have 40 per cent fewer calories. Xylitol also has a low glycaemic index (GI), which means that it has a low impact on blood sugar glucose levels, making it suitable for diabetics. It's advisable to use xylitol in small amounts until you are used to it, as it can have a mild laxative effect on some people. Studies have shown that xylitol can actually protect teeth from decay by up to 80 per cent if used as the sole sweetener in the diet.

Lucuma Powder

This is obtained from the lucuma (pronounced *lu-koo-ma*) fruit that originates from the Andean coastal valleys of Peru. Known as the 'gold of the Incas', it is said to have been one of their crops. It's a highly nutritious, full-bodied natural sweetener that contains high levels of carotene, B vitamins (in particular B3) and iron. Lucuma is the most popular ice cream flavour in Peru and tastes great added to sweet raw food dishes.

Lucuma Powder

Essential Oils

Minute quantities of therapeutic-grade essential oils not only taste stunning in raw chocolate recipes but actually carry health benefits too. In her vegan *Essential Oil Cookbook*, raw food exponent Menkit Prince refers to doctor and author Daniel Penoel MD, who recommends using these purest-quality oils in food preparation because they can enhance the immune system, purify the body and release 'feel-good' endorphins. American doctor Phillip Minton reports that consuming essential oils may protect against heart disease, cancer and dementia and improve circulation and oxygenation. It's vital that you consume only therapeutic-grade oils, as food-grade oils are usually inferior in quality (check with the manufacturer that they are safe to use in food). Once you have these oils, you can use them in all sorts of ways to enhance your wellbeing, including in your bath, as a massage oil or cleaning product and in burners.

Cautionary Note

I recommend seeking advice from an experienced aromatherapist when selecting essential oils to use as culinary ingredients. There are many different grades of essential oil available and ingesting essential oils is currently not a universally accepted practice.

Agave Nectar

This comes from a Mexican plant that looks similar to a cactus, and is the same plant that tequila comes from. It has taken a bit of a rap at the time of writing as a result of poor manufacturing processing due to the raised level of demand, so it's absolutely essential that you purchase only premium-quality, raw, light-coloured versions of the nectar – the dark variety is reportedly burned. As with all foods, moderation is the key here. I have used agave (pronounced *agar-vay*) nectar as part of a raw food diet. It works super synergistically with raw chocolate, as it's ultra sweet and light in texture.

Raw Nut & Seed Butters

These butters are made by grinding down the whole raw nut or seed using low-heat methods. You can purchase them ready made from health-food shops and some supermarkets, but they are also easy to make at home – *see* page 23 for a recipe. They taste great spread onto fruit or dehydrated crackers and added to smoothies, salad dressings, spreads or raw chocolate recipes. My favourites are raw almond butter, raw tahini (pulped sesame seeds) and raw cashew butter.

Dried Goji Berries

Also known as wolfberries, goji (pronounced *go-jee*) berries hit the headlines a few years ago when they became one of the best-selling health foods overnight, but I had been promoting the benefits of these fabulous little power berries for some years beforehand. They are also used in Traditional Chinese Medicine. Goji berries are particularly high in B vitamins (B1, B2 and B6), beta carotene, antioxidants and amino acids.

Dried Goji Berries

Hemp Seeds

Hemp seeds are one of my favourite seeds. They are highly nutritious and contain a full amino acid spectrum, meaning they are regarded as a complete protein. They offer an impressive trace mineral content and have a good balance of healthy omega-3 and omega-6 essential fatty acids.

Guarana Powder

Flax Seeds

Flax is grown on the Western Canadian Prairies especially for its seeds, which are rich in oil. It's a highly nutritious food that contains an important 'parent' omega-6 fatty acid that is the basic building bloc for all other omega-3 fatty acids. Flax seeds also contain omega-9 fatty acids, potassium, B vitamins, zinc, magnesium, lecithin, fibre and protein.

Raw Coconut Oil

Also known as coconut butter, coconut oil is a health food that's high in lauric acid, which is also present in breast milk. It's often solid at room temperature and may need to be warmed in a bain-marie or a dehydrator before using in my recipes (see page 20).

Maca Powder

This is another great staple Peruvian food that is steeped in history. Grown in the Andes between 3,300 metres/11,000 feet and 4,200 metres/14,000 feet, it's an incredibly powerful food with adaptogenic properties – helping to restore balance in the body. High in B vitamins (B1, B2 and B6), iron, potassium, calcium and zinc, it's classified as a complete protein, as it contains all the essential amino acids.

Guarana Powder

This should be avoided during pregnancy and breast-feeding. Guarana (pronounced *gwar-na*) is an evergreen climbing vine that is indigenous to the Amazonian basin. Considered to enhance energy and concentration, it's traditionally used to treat headaches, bacterial infections and fevers. It's also thought to be a sexual stimulant, so is used as an aphrodisiac.

Pink Crystal Salt

This is an alkalizing, naturally occurring salt that can actually be beneficial to your health in very small amounts. It's completely different from table salts and other types of refined salts, and can bring about genuine metabolic change within the body system.

Vanilla Pods

Vanilla pods were introduced to Europe by the same Spanish conquistador, Cortés, who introduced us to chocolate back in the sixteenth century (*see* page 10), which must be why vanilla and chocolate go hand in hand. They are best used by slicing lengthways down the centre with a very sharp knife, splitting open and scraping out the thousands of tiny black seeds.

Purple Corn Extract Powder

Yet another Peruvian wonder, this powder is traditionally made into a drink. I love to include tiny amounts in my raw chocolate recipes, as it's high in antioxidants and has such a beautiful vibrant colour.

Purple Corn Extract Powder

Making the Most of Raw Chocolate

Making your own raw chocolate dishes and sweet treats is a fun activity for everyone and one that we can all benefit from nutritionally. Whether you want to serve a home-made raw chocolate dessert to complement a wholesome main course or fancy making a batch of raw chocolate truffles to eat with your afternoon tea, the ways in which you can enjoy this fabulous food of the future are endless.

My raw chocolate recipes are suitable for almost everyone, including vegetarians, vegans, raw foodists, environmentalists and those on a gluten-free, wheat-free, sugar-free, egg-free or dairy-free diet. People with diabetes or hyperglycaemia or those who are on a calorie-controlled diet can also enjoy my recipes, although please take the sensible precaution of consulting your healthcare practitioner first if you have a medical condition.

Opting for Raw Plant Foods

Many people enjoy raw chocolate as part of a broader raw food diet. Huge health benefits can occur when we simply eat more raw plant-based food than cooked. It's one of the easiest ways to detoxify the system and live a healthier, more energized life. Increasing the percentage of raw plant foods in the diet to at least 60, 70 or even 80 per cent can help take your overall level of health to an all-time high. I do, however, recommend that you consult a fully qualified, raw food-friendly nutritional advisor before making fundamental changes to your diet.

Taking the Vegan Way

A growing number of people, from all walks of life, are choosing not to consume animals or their by-products for ethical, nutritional, environmental and spiritual reasons. My family and I enjoy a vegan diet and have never felt healthier and more connected to nature, at the same time knowing that fewer animals are having their lives sacrificed for the sake of humankind. This is naturally a healthier option for the environment too.

When to Avoid or Limit Raw Chocolate

Avoid eating raw chocolate during pregnancy, especially the first trimester, as it can have a stimulating effect. There have been no scientific studies carried out to examine whether raw chocolate consumption poses a risk to the mother or unborn child. Therefore, I think it's best to err on the side of caution. Seek your healthcare practitioner's advice before consuming raw chocolate, especially during the first trimester.

If you're pregnant, also avoid adding essential oils to the recipes for flavouring, but instead use the seeds scraped from vanilla pods (*see* page 17).

Also avoid consuming raw chocolate when you want sleep – due to the response that the naturally occurring chemical theobromine has on the adrenals (*see* page 13), eating raw chocolate may release feelings of euphoria and elation. Although this intense feeling is highly pleasurable, it's not so desirable when you want to get a good night's sleep.

Raw chocolate is a powerful and complex food, which may be too intense for the delicate systems of little people to deal with, so babies and children under three years old should avoid all types of chocolate products.

Preparing to Make Great Chocolate

I have clearly detailed all the unusual ingredients on pages 14–17 to make sourcing them as easy for you as possible. Shop around because the internet doesn't necessarily offer the best deals and some companies trade without ethics. Mail order is always an option for you. If your local health-food shop doesn't stock what you need, take this book down to show them and ask them to order the ingredients in for you, as they are all available through health-food wholesalers. Some supermarkets stock the ingredients too.

Foods such as raw nut and seed milks and flours (*see* page 23) as well as the biscuit-type Buckwheaties and Pink Buckwheaties (*see* page 22) form the foundation of many of my recipes, and can all be made in advance and stored accordingly. What's more, they can be used for creating all kinds of healthy dishes in addition to those in the book, and will soon become your trusty storecupboard staples.

Recipe Skill Levels

Easy peasy! These recipes are incredibly quick and simple to make, and are ideal ones to choose to get you on the raw chocolate road.

You can do it! These recipes also shouldn't take too long to make, especially if you have any basic recipes (*see* pages 22–3) that may be involved made up in advance and stored ready to use.

You pro! These are slightly more advanced recipes, which are sure to impress your friends and family. They may take slightly longer to make or involve some kind of technique to master.

  Easy peasy!

You can do it!

You pro!

Adding the Final Vital Ingredient

I'm a big believer that we should all try and make food with a positive energy – with love in our hearts and a smile on our faces – as this is the vital ingredient for healing and benefiting those who are going to be sharing the food that we make.

Raw Chocolate Equipment

The following is a concise guide to the equipment used throughout the book. A list of any special equipment appears with each recipe just above the ingredients list.

Power Blender

Food Processor

Power Blender & Plunger
Most recipes in this book will need a power blender. This is different to a regular smoothie maker or kitchen blender, which simply won't survive for long in processing the low water-content mixtures involved in the recipes. I own a Vitamix blender that also acts as a hob (it can heat food), a smoothie maker, kitchen blender, nut and seed grinder or coffee mill, ice cream maker, nut and seed milk maker and juicer. Use the plunger to push the ingredients towards the blade, especially the more solid, bulkier ones.

Power Blender Substitute
If you don't own a power blender, you could try adding the ingredients to your food processor first before transferring them to your regular blender jug.

Bain-marie
A bain-marie can be used to gently melt raw cacao butter to a runny liquid or to soften or melt raw coconut oil if it has hardened and turned white. Add the solid cacao butter or coconut oil to a heatproof glass bowl standing over a wide, shallow saucepan or frying pan of hot, rather than boiling, water on your hob's lowest heat setting. It should take about 10 minutes to melt the butter or oil until runny. Alternatively, you can use a dehydrator (*see* below).

Bain-Marie

Food Processor
Most people's kitchen cupboards have a food processor lurking at the back, but it's no use hiding it away gathering dust. They make life so much easier, especially if you own the sort with extra attachments that slice and grate your fruit and vegetables too.

Dehydrator
This item of raw food kitchen equipment is used to replicate the texture of oven-baked foods, such as crackers, biscuits and crêpes, while keeping their enzymes and nutrients intact. It works by slowly drying out the food in order to naturally preserve it, and as a

result intensifies the flavour. The Excalibur brand comes with mesh screens and sometimes ParaFlexx Sheets (solid non-stick sheets) too, which fit the square trays perfectly. The dehydrator can also be used to gently melt raw cacao butter or coconut oil. Place in a small dish and leave on one of the dehydrator shelves at 40.5°C/105°F for around 15–20 minutes or until melted.

Dehydrator

Dehydrator Substitute

If you don't have a dehydrator, you can use your oven on the lowest heat setting and place the food that you wish to dehydrate on a non-metal tray. This method isn't environmentally friendly, so you may decide to double the batch size to make it more worthwhile or invest in a dehydrator when you begin to see how useful they are.

Silicone Chocolate/Cake Moulds
& BPA-free Plastic Containers

Silicone chocolate and cake moulds are ideal for giving home-made raw chocolate items a professional look with an attractive glossy finish. If you don't have silicone moulds, you can always use BPA-free plastic containers instead (*see* right).

Jessica's top kitchen tips

- Before you start, use a plant-based, chemical-free, environmentally sound worktop sanitizer that hasn't been tested on animals.
- Water and raw chocolate don't mix well, so keep your equipment dry. It helps to have a pile of tea towels on hand exclusively for this job.
- Wash up using an environmentally sound washing-up liquid. I find it easier to wash up as I go along, to avoid my kitchen looking like a disaster zone.
- If you prepare meat or their by-products in your kitchen, be sure to use separate cleaning cloths and washing-up brushes for cleaning your raw chocolate utensils.

What is BPA?

Most polycarbonate plastic containers and drinks bottles contain an industrial chemical called bisphenol-A, or BPA. BPA is oestrogenic, that is it promotes or mimics the action of female hormones, and recent studies have raised doubts about its safety.

Basic Recipes

This is a selection of recipes that can be made in advance and used to make many of the dishes in this book. If you don't own a dehydrator you can use your oven on the lowest heat setting instead.

Buckwheaties

Buckwheaties can be made in large batches and kept in an airtight container in your kitchen cupboard. They are really useful to have in store, as they give a fantastic crunch when mixed with many recipes. They always come in handy for sprinkling over ice cream and adding to cake bases, chocolates and breakfast cereals, as well as for decorating cakes or simply eating by the handful.

MAKES 1 KG/2 LB 4 OZ

EQUIPMENT
- **dehydrator with solid dehydrator sheets**

INGREDIENTS
- **1 kg/2 lb 4 oz raw buckwheat groats**
- **1.5–2 litres/2¾–3½ pints fresh filtered water**

1 Soak your buckwheat groats by leaving them in a large sieve fully immersed in a large bowl containing the filtered water. Leave to soak for 2–4 hours.

2 Drain off the soaking water, which should be gloopy in texture and pink in colour. Leave the groats standing in the sieve in your kitchen sink to fully drain and begin the germination process, which lasts until the following day. You may start to see little tails appear on your groats, which is normal, as they are sprouting. Don't let the tails get longer than half the length of a groat, as you may find that their taste changes and they become quite bitter – leave them to drain from between 1 hour and up to overnight, but no longer than that.

3 Spoon the groats onto the solid paraflex dehydrator sheets in thin layers and then dehydrate at 40.5°C/105°F until the morning, or for 8–12 hours.

4 Stored in an airtight glass jar. They keep for months, although in my house they're eaten after a few days!

Buckwheaties

Pink Buckwheaties

Pink is by far my favourite colour and always makes me feel great, so I invented this brightly coloured variation on the plain Buckwheaties recipe for sprinkling over dishes. You can also use these anywhere in place of plain Buckwheaties, although just remember that if you choose to add the peppermint essential oil, be careful that the hint of mint doesn't clash with other flavours.

MAKES 1 KG/2 LB 4 OZ

EQUIPMENT
- **power blender**
- **dehydrator with solid dehydrator sheets**

INGREDIENTS
- **85 g/3 oz peeled beetroot**
- **6 tbsp freshly squeezed orange juice**
- **90 g/3¼ oz raw agave nectar**
- **4 drops peppermint essential oil (optional)**
- **1 kg/2 lb 4 oz Buckwheaties (see left)**

1 Add all the ingredients, except the Buckwheaties, to your power blender jug and blend on full power, using the plunger, until smooth.

2 Place the prepared Buckwheaties in a mixing bowl and pour the contents of your blender jug over the groats. Stir in the liquid thoroughly with a spoon until the pink liquid is evenly distributed and covers all the groats.

3 Spoon the Buckwheaties onto the solid dehydrator sheets and flatten with the back of a spoon until they are just one layer thick. Place in your dehydrator on a medium-height shelf and dehydrate at 40.5°C/105°F for 12–15 hours or until crispy.

4 Store in an airtight glass jar in a cool, dark place. They will last for over a month.

Raw Nut & Seed Milk

This is a generic recipe for using a variety of unsalted raw nuts and seeds, but choose a single type at any one time. Almonds, cashew nuts, Brazil nuts, hulled hemp seeds and sunflower seeds work best in my experience.

MAKES 1 LITRE/1¾ PINTS OR 4 MEDIUM-SIZED GLASSES

EQUIPMENT
- **powder blender**
- **organic muslin square**
- **large jug**

INGREDIENTS
- **150 g/5½ oz your favourite unsalted raw nuts or seeds (choose one type)**
- **1 litre/1¾ pints fresh filtered water**
- **yacon syrup or raw agave nectar, for sweetening (optional)**

1 Soak your nuts or seeds in a bowlful of fresh filtered water for between 15 minutes and overnight. You then need to drain the nuts or seeds and throw away the soaking water (it shouldn't be reused).

2 Add the nuts or seeds to your power blender along with the measured amount of fresh filtered water and blend on full power until they are completely broken down and the jug is full of white milk. When you slow the blender down, if you can hear stray nuts or seeds rattling around in the base of the blender jug, just give them another high-powered blast.

3 Drape the organic muslin square in a single layer over a large jug and push it down into the jug to create a pocket large enough to accommodate at least 500 ml/ 18 fl oz milk. Secure to the jug rim with a thick rubber band. Pour about half the milk into the muslin pocket and then use a tablespoon to stir the milk and encourage it to trickle through the muslin into the jug.

4 When the first half of the milk has trickled through, tip the rest of the milk from the blender jug into the muslin pocket and then carefully remove the rubber band, ensuring that the muslin stays over the jug at all times. Firmly hold the muslin above the bulging pouch of milk with one hand while you squeeze the pouch with the other hand. As the pouch of milk reduces in size, start to twist and wring the muslin, still firmly holding the top of the pouch in one hand to stop the milk and pulp from spilling.

5 Keep twisting and squeezing the muslin until the milk has stopped pouring out. You can freeze the pulp for later use. However, if you are using whole hemp seeds, you must discard the pulp.

6 Taste the milk and decide for yourself if it needs to be sweetened. If you feel it does, add a natural liquid sweetener such as yacon syrup or raw agave nectar. Start off with a small amount and then add more to taste. Babies and young children are often quite happy to consume the milk unsweetened.

Raw Nut and Seed Flour

You'll see that various nuts and seeds are milled to a flour in my recipes, to act as a healthy and nutritious base or thickener.

MAKES 500 G/1 LB 2 OZ

EQUIPMENT
- **power blender**

INGREDIENTS
- **500 g/1 lb 2 oz your chosen unsalted raw nuts or seeds, such as hulled hemp seeds, cashew nuts or almonds (choose one type)**

1 Add the nuts or seeds to your power blender and blend on full power, using the plunger, until they form a fine flour. This is best done in 2 batches.

2 Transfer to an airtight glass jar and store in your refrigerator for up to 3 months.

Raw Nut & Seed Butter

It's very easy to make your own raw nut or seed butters, but if you're short of time you can buy them from health-food shops.

MAKES 250 G/9 OZ

EQUIPMENT
- **power blender**

INGREDIENTS
- **250 g/9 oz your chosen unsalted raw nuts or seeds**

1 Add the nuts or seeds to your power blender and blend thoroughly on full power, using the plunger, until they form firstly a flour and then a butter.

2 Spoon into an airtight glass jar and store in your refrigerator for up to 3 months.

The Recipes

Raw Chocochino

When it's cold outside and you desire a beverage that will not only warm you from the inside out but also give you a mild kick, then my Raw Chocochino has to be it. It's thick, creamy, smooth and satisfying.

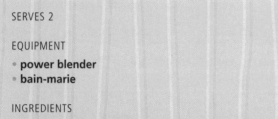

SERVES 2

EQUIPMENT
- **power blender**
- **bain-marie**

INGREDIENTS
- **500 ml/18 fl oz raw almond milk (*see* Raw Nut and Seed Milk, page 23)**
- **4 tbsp raw cacao powder**
- **85 g/3 oz raw agave nectar**
- **2 tsp raw cacao butter, grated or finely chopped**
- **5 drops vanilla essential oil**

1 Add the almond milk to your power blender jug with all the other ingredients. If you have the almond milk already made and sweetened in the refrigerator, just omit or add less agave nectar.

2 Blend on full power until you achieve a smooth, even consistency.

3 Heat the mixture gently using a bain-marie (*see* page 20), stirring the drink regularly and checking that it's not heating up too much (which would destroy the enzymes and nutrients), until warmed through but not hot.

4 Pour into beautiful cups and serve with matching saucers for a cute, kitsch, warming drink.

Cacao + Coconut Water Shake

Whether you're looking for a filling, nutritious start to your day or a post work-out snack, this is the recipe for you. I love the way that this shake leaves me feeling satisfied and unbelievably energized.

SERVES 2

EQUIPMENT
- **power blender**

INGREDIENTS
- **½ avocado, peeled**
- **350 ml/12 fl oz raw coconut water**
- **3 tbsp raw cacao powder**
- **10 fresh dates, stoned**
- **5 average-sized ice cubes**

1 Add all the ingredients to your power blender and blend on full power until smooth.

2 Pour into 2 glasses and add colourful straws and cocktail umbrellas. Drink straight away for a cool, filling and refreshing shake.

Jessica's top tip
Instead of adding vanilla essential oil, try sprinkling ground cinnamon over the Chocochino once served.

Cacao Maca Boost

My husband Tom and I thought it would be fun to create a shot-style drink that could be used in place of spirits when you're looking for a natural, healthy high, since neither of us drink alcohol. The raw cacao and maca work together on a heightened level to give you a boost in a far more intense and satisfying way than alcohol. This should be drunk immediately after making.

SERVES 2

EQUIPMENT

- **bain-marie or dehydrator**
- **power blender**
- **two 50-ml/2-fl oz shot glasses**

INGREDIENTS

- **3 tsp raw coconut oil**
- **100 ml/3½ fl oz raw almond milk, preferably unsweetened (see Raw Nut and Seed Milk, page 23)**
- **1 tbsp raw cacao powder**
- **1 tbsp raw agave nectar**
- **½ tsp raw maca powder**

Jessica's top tip
If you want an extra kick, add more maca powder to the blender, but be warned – it's potent stuff. Therefore, I would recommend that you initially keep to the quantities specified.

1 If the coconut oil is too firm to blend, melt it down gently into a soft or runny consistency in a bain-marie or dehydrator (see pages 20–1).
2 Add the coconut oil to your power blender with all the other ingredients and blend on full power until smooth.
3 Pour into the 2 shot glasses, then clink them together, say 'cheers' and knock back!

Choctail Mocktail

This non-alcoholic cocktail is prepared in a similar way to a conventional cocktail by using a cocktail shaker, and the raw cacao beans with skins will give you a real buzz. I like to sprinkle a pinch of raw cacao powder over the top to decorate it when I'm serving it at one of my parties or raw food events. It's one of those beverages that feels truly decadent and luxurious to drink.

SERVES 1

EQUIPMENT

- **power blender**
- **cocktail shaker**
- **martini glass**

INGREDIENTS

- **30 g/1 oz raw cacao beans**
- **250 ml/9 fl oz your favourite Raw Nut and Seed Milk (see page 23)**
- **25 g/1 oz dried goji berries**
- **40 g/1½ oz yacon syrup**
- **handful of crushed ice**

Jessica's top tips
I like to use milk made from hulled hemp seeds for this drink for a super-seed boost. When you double strain your drink, save the pulp for a sauce or a breakfast smoothie.

1 Add all the ingredients, except the crushed ice, to your power blender and blend on full power until smooth.
2 Add the crushed ice to the cocktail shaker, pour over the drink mixture and shake thoroughly before double straining into a martini glass. Drink straight away.

Raw Chocolate + Banana Smoothie

If we fancy a raw chocolate breakfast, this is usually what my husband or I will make. Although to be honest it's usually me who performs this task, so I'm grateful that it's such a quick and easy recipe. I even manage to make it these days while I step over chocolate moulds and cake tins as our son busily unpacks the kitchen cupboards.

SERVES 2

EQUIPMENT
- **power blender**

INGREDIENTS
- **3 large bananas, peeled**
- **2 tbsp raw cacao powder**
- **300 ml/10 fl oz fresh filtered water**
- **2 tsp raw almond butter**
  (*see* **Raw Nut and Seed Butter, page 23**)
- **5 fresh, juicy dates, such as Medjool, stoned**

1 Add all the ingredients to your power blender and blend on full power, using the plunger, until smooth.
2 Pour into 2 large glasses and serve immediately.

Jessica's top tip
I recommend drinking this smoothie straight away because of the inclusion of fresh banana, as they don't fare that well after they have been peeled.

Winter Warming Drinking Chocolate

On a cold winter's day when I want something warm to drink, but also want to stay as raw as possible to maintain high levels of energy and radiant health, I like to reach for this drink. It only takes a few minutes to make and it isn't overly sweet – you get that bitter, high-cacao content kick instead. But if you want to make it sweeter, just add a touch more yacon syrup.

SERVES 2

EQUIPMENT
- **bain-marie or dehydrator**
- **power blender**

INGREDIENTS
- **30 g/1 oz raw coconut oil**
- **500 ml/18 fl oz your favourite Raw Nut and Seed Milk (*see* page 23) – I like to use hulled hemp seeds**
- **4 tbsp raw cacao powder**
- **70 g/2½ oz yacon syrup**
- **1 tsp mixed spice**
- **1-cm/½-inch piece fresh ginger, peeled**

1 If the coconut oil is too firm to blend, melt it down gently into a soft or runny consistency in a bain-marie or dehydrator (*see* pages 20–1).
2 Add the coconut oil to your power blender with all the other ingredients and blend on full power, using the plunger, until smooth.
3 Pour the mixture into a glass mixing bowl and heat in the bain-marie until warm, stirring frequently. Pour into 2 favourite mugs and enjoy straight away.

Raw Chocolate-coated Brazils

My dad had an unhealthy obsession with chocolate-coated Brazil nuts. I told him that life's too short to scoff chocolates filled with refined sugar and dairy, and then swiftly invented a healthier alternative for him that I would love to share with you too.

MAKES ONE 450-G/1-LB LOAF TIN OF
CHOCOLATE-COATED BRAZIL NUT PIECES

EQUIPMENT

- **bain-marie or dehydrator**
- **power blender**
- **450-g/1-lb loaf tin**
- **stainless-steel hand whisk**

INGREDIENTS

- **150 g/5½ oz raw cacao butter**
- **425 g/15 oz raw Brazil nuts**
- **6 tbsp raw cacao powder**
- **150 g/5½ oz raw agave nectar**
- **4 pinches of cayenne pepper**
- **pinch of pink crystal salt**

Jessica's nutritional tip

Brazil nuts are high in magnesium and vitamin B1, and are made up of 13 per cent carbohydrate, 69 per cent fat and 18 per cent protein.

1 Melt the cacao butter gently in a bain-marie or dehydrator until runny (*see pages 20–1*).

2 Put 100 g/3½ oz of the Brazil nuts in your power blender and process on full power, using the plunger, until they form a fine flour. Add to a large mixing bowl along with all the other ingredients, except the remaining whole Brazil nuts. Spread the whole Brazil nuts out over the base of the loaf tin.

3 Using the hand whisk, gently mix the ingredients in the mixing bowl together until you have a smooth chocolate liquid with no visible lumps.

4 Pour the runny chocolate over the whole Brazil nuts in the loaf tin and use a dessertspoon to help mix the raw chocolate through. Gently shake the tin from side to side to ensure that the chocolate seals around the edge and then bang the base of the tin firmly against the work surface a few times to help any air bubbles rise to the top.

5 Place the tin in the freezer for around 30 minutes or until the chocolate has properly set.

6 Tip the loaf tin upside down on a chopping board and gently bang down until the heavy block of chocolate-coated Brazils falls out. Chop the block into small pieces using a very sharp knife and enjoy with a good book. Store in an airtight glass jar in the refrigerator for up 3–4 weeks.

Raw Cacao Fudge

If you like soft, fudge-like chocolate, then you'll love this – and it's really easy to make. I prepare it for presents for the wonderful people who cross my path when I want to say 'thank you', or just because I feel like it. After I've popped the fudge pieces out of the mould, I put several in a recycled paper box, lined with greaseproof paper, and tie with a colourful piece of ribbon – the perfect raw chocolate gift. Alternatively, enjoy them yourself with a loved one – or anyone in fact!

MAKES 16 PIECES

EQUIPMENT
- **bain-marie or dehydrator**
- **power blender**
- **16-hole silicone chocolate mould or shallow, medium-sized BPA-free plastic container**

INGREDIENTS
- **250 g/9 oz raw cacao paste**
- **75 g/2¾ oz raw cacao butter**
- **2 tbsp lecithin granules**
- **175 g/6 oz raw agave nectar**
- **8–10 drops vanilla essential oil**
- **pinch of pink crystal salt**

1 Melt the cacao paste and butter gently together in a bain-marie or dehydrator until runny (*see* pages 20–1).

2 Add the melted cacao paste and butter with all the other ingredients to your power blender jug and blend thoroughly on full power, using the plunger, until smooth.

3 Spoon the mixture evenly into the holes of the mould – you can choose whichever shape you fancy. But if you are in a rush, just spoon it into a medium-sized BPA-free plastic container no more than 2 cm/¾ inch deep. Freeze for 1 hour or until your fudge is nice and firm.

4 Take the mould out of the freezer and pop the fudge pieces out onto a chopping board. If you have used a container, turn the block of fudge out and then use a very sharp knife to carefully slice it into cubes. Store in an airtight glass jar in the refrigerator for up to 3–4 weeks.

Jessica's top tip
Try adding a few drops of orange essential oil instead of the vanilla essential oil for an authentic chocolate-orange taste.

Tangy Lemon Chocolates

Raw chocolate is so versatile and makes a great base for you to be as creative as you like. So here, if you don't have any lemon essential oil, you could substitute it for another safe-to-consume organic essential oil instead, or simply omit it from the recipe altogether. I like enjoying these chocolates on a warm summer's day, as the tangy flavours dancing in my mouth echo the joys of summertime itself.

MAKES 26 CHOCOLATES

EQUIPMENT
- **bain-marie or dehydrator**
- **power blender**
- **two 16-hole silicone chocolate moulds or one medium-sized BPA-free plastic container**

INGREDIENTS
- **100 g/3½ oz raw cacao butter**
- **75 g/2¾ oz raw hulled hemp seeds**
- **3 heaped tbsp raw cacao powder**
- **4 heaped tsp xylitol crystals**
- **4 drops lemon essential oil**
- **25 g/1 oz Buckwheaties (see page 22)**
- **pinch of pink crystal salt**

1 Melt the cacao butter gently in a bain-marie or dehydrator until runny (*see pages 20–1*).

2 Process the hemp seeds in your power blender on full power, using the plunger, until they form a fine flour. Use a butter knife or chopstick to scrape the milled seeds away from the base and side of the blender jug if they have stuck.

3 Add the melted cacao butter with all the other ingredients to the milled seeds in the power blender and blend thoroughly on full power, using the plunger, until you have a thick, melted chocolate consistency.

4 Using a teaspoon, carefully spoon the chocolate mixture into each hole of the mould. If you don't have a chocolate mould, use a medium-sized BPA-free plastic container instead.

5 When each hole is evenly filled, shift the mould or container from side to side on your kitchen work surface and firmly bang it down a few times to release any air bubbles.

6 Place in the freezer for about 30 minutes or until your chocolates are firm.

7 Turn the mould upside down on a chopping board and pop each chocolate out. If you have used a plastic container, turn the block of chocolate out and use a very sharp knife to cut it into bite-sized pieces. Store in an airtight glass jar in the refrigerator for up to 3–4 weeks.

Fresh Cherry + Chocolate Truffles

I think there is something ridiculously delectable about cherries and chocolate. It's time to take this pleasure to the next level by using fresh, sweet, ripe organic cherries combined with antioxidant-rich, organic raw chocolate – ooh la la! Could life get any sweeter?

MAKES ABOUT 24 SMALL SQUARES

EQUIPMENT

- **bain-marie or dehydrator**
- **power blender**
- **medium-sized square BPA-free plastic container**

INGREDIENTS

- **150 g/5½ oz raw cacao butter**
- **12 fresh, ripe cherries, washed**
- **100 g/3½ oz whole raw almonds**
- **55 g/2 oz raw cacao powder**
- **5 tbsp xylitol crystals**
- **100 g/3½ oz yacon syrup**
- **pinch of pink crystal salt**

Jessica's top tip

Use an 18-cm/7-inch square plastic container to set the chocolate in for this recipe, as it's the perfect size to create these melt-in-the-mouth, chunky truffles.

1 Melt the cacao butter gently in a bain-marie or dehydrator until runny (see pages 20–1).

2 Meanwhile, stop picking at the cherries or there will be none left! Halve and stone them and then put to one side.

3 Process the almonds in your power blender on full power, using the plunger, until they form a fine flour. Use a butter knife or chopstick to scrape the milled nuts away from the base and side of the blender jug if they have stuck.

4 Add the cacao butter, cacao powder, xylitol crystals, yacon syrup and salt to the blender and blend on full power, using the plunger, until you have a smooth and creamy chocolate mixture.

5 Pour into your plastic container and place in the freezer for 15 minutes to begin the setting process.

6 Dry the cherry halves between the layers of a folded tea towel – for the chocolate to set, it's essential that they don't carry any excess moisture.

7 Retrieve the container of semi-hard chocolate from the freezer for a moment while you sprinkle the cherries over the top. If needs be, gently push them a little way into the chocolate so that they are firmly held. Return the container to the freezer for a further 20 minutes or until the chocolate has properly set hard.

8 Tip your container upside down onto a chopping board and pop the block of chocolate truffle out. Using a very sharp knife, cut into 2-cm/¾-inch squares. Keep refrigerated in an airtight glass jar and bear in mind that the fresh cherries will go off if they aren't eaten within a few days, which gives you a great excuse to devour the lot. Alternatively, after you have sliced them into squares, you could put them back in the freezer, where they will keep for a few weeks.

White + Dark Orange Creams

This recipe makes a selection of beautifully shiny, two-tone chocolates, which I created in the first instance to decorate my raw chocolate wedding cake. In spite of their exotic looks, they are actually quite easy to make. I'm a real fan of orange essential oil, but you could try others such as lemon, peppermint or cinnamon – or even chilli if you're feeling adventurous.

MAKES 20 CREAMS

EQUIPMENT

- **power blender**
- **bain-marie or dehydrator**
- **one 20-hole or two 16-hole silicone chocolate moulds**

INGREDIENTS

- **100 g/3½ oz raw cashew nuts**
- **3 tbsp xylitol crystals**
- **2 tbsp raw coconut oil**
- **4–6 drops orange essential oil**
- **90 g/3¼ oz raw cacao butter**
- **40 g/1½ oz raw whole almonds**
- **1 vanilla pod, split in half lengthways and seeds scraped out**
- **1 tbsp lecithin granules**
- **60 g/2¼ oz raw agave nectar**
- **3 tbsp raw cacao powder**
- **pinch of pink crystal salt**

Jessica's top tip

It's best to be sure that the orange cream layer has completely set before adding the chocolate layer, otherwise it will be impossible to get a straight line between the two flavours.

1 Add the cashew nuts to your power blender jug along with the xylitol crystals and process together on full power, using the plunger, until they form a fine flour. Use a butter knife or chopstick to scrape the milled mixture away from the base and side of the blender jug if stuck.

2 If the coconut oil is too firm to blend, melt it down gently into a soft or runny consistency in a bain-marie or dehydrator (see pages 20–1). Add it to your blender with the orange essential oil and blend on full power, using the plunger.

3 Take 2 teaspoons and use one to spoon half a teaspoonful of the orange cream from the blender. Use the handle end of the other teaspoon to help push the mixture off the spoon and directly into the base of one hole of the mould. Continue until you have used up all the mixture. Place the mould or moulds in the freezer for about 15 minutes until firm and set while you make the dark chocolate part.

4 Melt the cacao butter gently in a bain-marie or dehydrator until runny (see pages 20–1).

5 Add the almonds, vanilla seeds and lecithin granules to your power blender and process the ingredients together into a fine flour, as before.

6 Add the melted cacao butter with the rest of the ingredients to the almond mixture in the blender and blend on full power, using the plunger, until runny and smooth.

7 Take the mould or moulds out of the freezer. Add 1–2 teaspoons of the runny chocolate mixture directly on top of the orange creams and then return to the freezer for 10–15 minutes until firm and set.

8 Remove the chocolates from the freezer and pop them carefully out of the mould or moulds. Store in an airtight jar in the refrigerator for up to 3–4 weeks.

Double-dunked Raw Chocolate Truffles

Try these truffles if you want a rich, full-bodied raw chocolate experience. Soft and melt-in-the-mouth, they are coated in cacao powder and then dipped in a Chocolicious Sauce and sprinkled with crunchy Pink Buckwheaties.

MAKES 38 TRUFFLES

EQUIPMENT

- **bain-marie or dehydrator**
- **food processor**
- **stainless-steel hand whisk**
- **solid dehydrator sheet**

INGREDIENTS

- **115 g/4 oz raw cacao butter**
- **175 g/6 oz raw cashew nuts**
- **6–8 drops vanilla essential oil**
- **150 ml/5 fl oz fresh filtered water**
- **125 g/4½ oz stoned and peeled avocado**
- **6 heaped tbsp raw cacao powder, plus 3 tbsp for coating**
- **1 tsp lucuma powder**
- **125 g/4½ oz raw agave nectar**
- **pinch of pink crystal salt**
- **Pink Buckwheaties (see page 22), for sprinkling (optional but highly recommended)**

Chocolicious sauce
(optional but highly recommended)
- **100 g/3½ oz raw cacao butter**
- **6 tbsp raw cacao powder**
- **85 g/3 oz raw agave nectar**

1 Melt the cacao butter gently in a bain-marie or dehydrator until runny (see pages 20–1).

2 Process the cashew nuts and vanilla essential oil with the water in your food processor until the nuts are broken into small pieces. Add the avocado and process again until the mixture turns green.

3 Add the cacao powder, the lucuma powder, agave nectar, salt and melted cacao butter to the food processor and then process once more until all ingredients are thoroughly blended. Spoon into a medium-sized glass bowl and place, uncovered, in the freezer for 20 minutes or until the mixture has firmed up a little.

4 Remove from the freezer and, using a teaspoon, spoon a small amount of the mixture into the palm of your hand. Sprinkle a teaspoonful of the cacao powder for coating over the truffle and then roll it between your palms into a ball. Repeat with the remaining mixture and cacao powder. Place the truffles in the freezer, covered in foil, for at least 30 minutes.

5 When the truffles have firmed up a little, remove from the freezer and very gently roll each one in your palms again to smooth them over.

6 For the optional Chocolicious Sauce coating, melt the cacao butter as before.

7 When the cacao butter has fully melted, spoon in the cacao powder before pouring in the agave nectar. Using the hand whisk, gently whisk the mixture until the powder and liquids are fully combined.

8 Take the glass mixing bowl out of the pan of hot water. Add each truffle one at a time to the sauce, using a fork in each hand to roll it through the chocolate, until completely coated, then lift out the truffle and place directly onto a solid dehydrator sheet. Swiftly repeat this process while the sauce remains warm until all your truffles are evenly coated. Place the dehydrator sheet on a tray and transfer to your refrigerator for about 30 minutes for the chocolate coating to set enough to be double dunked.

9 Remove the truffles from the refrigerator and repeat step 8. Sprinkle the truffles with Pink Buckwheaties (as much or as little as you like), if using. Place the dehydrator sheet on a tray and transfer to your refrigerator for about 2 hours to make them firm throughout. The truffles will keep in an airtight glass jar in the refrigerator for up to 2 weeks.

Cinnamon-flavoured Raw Chocolate Bars

I'm a big fan of giving at Christmas time, as well as on the other 364 days of the year, and making raw chocolate bars that capture the classic flavours of Christmas for those around me during this celebration of love seems to make perfect sense. What's the point in giving chocolates to a loved one that may damage their health and therefore mar their happiness in the long run? So why not try replacing junk confectionery with this home-made raw, antioxidant-fuelled chocolate when you feel the need to give someone a special sweet something.

MAKES 18 BARS

EQUIPMENT

- bain-marie or dehydrator
- power blender
- two 12-hole polycarbonate professional chocolate bar moulds
- icing pen (optional)

INGREDIENTS

White chocolate decoration
- 40 g/1½ oz raw cacao butter
- 30 g/1 oz raw cashew nuts
- 1 heaped tsp xylitol crystals

Chocolate bars
- 280 g/10 oz raw cacao butter
- 6 tbsp raw cacao powder
- 100 g/3½ oz raw agave nectar
- 8–10 drops cinnamon essential oil
- pinch of pink crystal salt

1 For the white chocolate decoration, melt the cacao butter gently in a bain-marie or dehydrator until runny (*see* pages 20–1).

2 Add the cashew nuts to your power blender and blend on full power, using the plunger, until they form a fine flour. Use a butter knife or chopstick to scrape away the milled nuts from the base and side of the blender jug if they have stuck.

3 Add the melted cacao butter and xylitol crystals to the milled nuts in the blender and blend on full power, using the plunger, until you have a thick, melted chocolate consistency.

4 Using a teaspoon, carefully spoon out a small amount of the white chocolate from your blender jug and pour it in thin stripes over the holes of the bar mould in a zigzag pattern. If you want the decoration to look really professional, you could use an icing pen instead, which creates a much steadier line. Don't let the white chocolate cover too much of the surface area, as you want it to remain a pattern on the top of the chocolate bars. Place on a flat surface in the freezer and cover with foil while you prepare the chocolate bar mixture.

5 For the chocolate bars, melt the cacao butter as before. Add to your power blender jug with all the other ingredients and blend on full power until you have a thick, chocolatey texture.

6 Remove the moulds from the freezer, spoon 2–3 tablespoons of the mixture into each hole on top of the white chocolate decoration and level the surface. Don't worry – you will *see* the attractive decorations that you designed again when it's time to pop the chocolate out of the moulds. Shift the moulds from side to side and then bang firmly down on your work surface a few times to expel any air bubbles. Return to the freezer, covered with foil, for 30–60 minutes or until the chocolate has firmly set.

7 When you are sure that the raw chocolate has set hard, bang the base of each mould in turn firmly on your work surface a few times to loosen the chocolate bars, then tip upside down over a chopping board and twist the mould, holding an end in each hand, in opposite directions – towards the ceiling and floor. This will loosen the seal between the mould and the chocolate, allowing the bars to fall out onto the board. Turn your raw chocolate bars over and stare in amazement at the beautifully designed bars that you have created. Store in an airtight BPA-free plastic container in the refrigerator for up to a month.

Peppermint Creams

What recipe book of sweet pleasures would be complete without a mouth-watering peppermint cream recipe for you to enjoy? For the first time ever, you can enjoy this popular chocolate in its healthiest and most energy-generating state. When you bite through the crisp shell into the peppermint layer, you might just collapse on the floor in a heap of total bliss that only the life-enhancing effects of raw chocolate provides.

MAKES 28 PEPPERMINT CREAMS

EQUIPMENT
- **bain-marie or dehydrator**
- **food processor**
- **stainless-steel hand whisk**
- **solid dehydrator sheet**

INGREDIENTS
- **125 g/4½ oz raw cacao butter**
- **175 g/6 oz raw cashew nuts**
- **10 drops peppermint essential oil**
- **50 ml/2 fl oz fresh filtered water**
- **150 g/5½ oz stoned and peeled avocado**
- **1 tsp lucuma powder**
- **100 g/3½ oz raw agave nectar or 50 g/1¾ oz yacon syrup**
- **2 tsp xylitol crystals (or 4 tsp if using yacon syrup)**
- **pinch of pink crystal salt**
- **3 tbsp raw cacao powder**
- **Pink Buckwheaties (see page 22), for sprinkling (optional but highly recommended)**

Chocolicious sauce
- **100 g/3½ oz raw cacao butter**
- **6 tbsp raw cacao powder**
- **85 g/3 oz raw agave nectar**

1 Melt the cacao butter gently in a bain-marie or dehydrator until runny (*see pages 20–1*).

2 Process the cashew nuts and peppermint essential oil with the water in your food processor until the nuts are broken into small pieces. Add the avocado and process again until the mixture turns green.

3 Add the lucuma powder, agave nectar, xylitol crystals, salt and melted cacao butter to the food processor and then process once more until all ingredients are thoroughly blended. Spoon into a medium-sized glass bowl and place, uncovered, in the freezer for 30 minutes or until the mixture has firmed up a little.

4 Remove from the freezer and, using a teaspoon, spoon a small amount of the mixture into the palm of your hand. Roll it between your palms into a ball. Repeat with the remaining mixture. Place the plate of peppermint creams in the freezer, covered in foil, while you prepare the Chocolicious Sauce for coating.

5 Melt the cacao butter as before.

6 When the cacao butter has fully melted, spoon in the cacao powder before pouring in the agave nectar. Using the hand whisk, gently whisk the mixture until the powder and liquids are fully combined.

7 Remove the peppermint creams from the freezer. Take the glass mixing bowl out of the pan of hot water. Add each peppermint cream one at a time to the sauce, using a fork to roll it through the chocolate, until completely coated. Use the fork to scoop out the chocolate-coated peppermint cream and place directly onto a solid dehydrator sheet. Swiftly repeat this process while the sauce remains warm until all your peppermint creams are evenly coated. Sprinkle with Pink Buckwheaties (as much or as little as you like), if using. Place the dehydrator sheet on a tray and transfer to your refrigerator for about 30 minutes for the chocolate coating to set, but refrigerate for up to 2 hours to make them firm throughout. The peppermint creams will keep in an airtight glass jar in the refrigerator for up to 2 weeks.

Ginger Caramels

I don't tell people to expect a caramel centre in these chocolates when they try them for the first time, as I love the expression on their faces when they discover it for themselves. The explosion of melting ginger caramel and raw chocolate is almost too good to be true.

MAKES 15 CARAMELS

EQUIPMENT

- bain-marie or dehydrator
- power blender
- 16-hole silicone chocolate mould

INGREDIENTS

- 4 tbsp yacon syrup
- 2 drops ginger essential oil
- 90 g/3¼ oz raw cacao butter
- 40 g/1½ oz raw cashew nuts
- 4 tbsp raw cacao powder
- 2 tbsp xylitol crystals
- 2 tbsp lucuma powder
- 4 drops vanilla essential oil
- pinch of pink crystal salt

Jessica's top tip

Make this recipe when you have the time to master the technique involved in filling each chocolate. It's not complex, but it may take some practice if you are using very narrow moulds.

1 For the ginger caramel centres, put the yacon syrup in a small dish and stir in the ginger essential oil using a dessertspoon. Place in the freezer to firm up while you prepare the chocolate. Don't worry that the yacon syrup will freeze – it just becomes firm, making it much easier to work with.

2 Melt the cacao butter gently in a bain-marie or dehydrator until runny (see pages 20–1).

3 Process the cashew nuts in your power blender on full power, using the plunger, until they form a fine flour. Use a butter knife or chopstick to scrape the milled nuts away from the base and side of the blender jug if they have stuck.

4 Add the melted cacao butter and all the remaining ingredients to your power blender jug and blend on full power, using the plunger until you achieve a smooth, runny texture.

5 Carefully spoon a teaspoonful of the chocolate mixture into each hole of the mould, and then set the remaining chocolate aside. Transfer the mould to the freezer for at least 10 minutes or until completely firm.

6 Remove the mould from the freezer, along with the dish of ginger caramel. Using a butter knife, drizzle a small amount of ginger caramel directly into the centre of each solid chocolate. It's important not to let the caramel touch the sides of the mould as you do this, otherwise it will start to seep out.

7 With the caramel sitting in the centres of the solid chocolates, quickly pour a dessertspoonful of the reserved runny chocolate over each, covering them completely. Place the mould back in the freezer for at least 10 minutes until set.

8 Once the chocolate has set, carefully pop each ginger caramel out of the mould and onto a plate. These chocolates are best stored in the refrigerator for up to 3–4 weeks in an airtight glass jar and enjoyed on a cool day with a Raw Chocochino (see page 26).

Almond Butter Truffles

This is a great quick and easy recipe if you don't have access to a power blender such as when you are travelling. If I'm in a warm climate, I let the sun melt the cacao butter for me as I prepare the other ingredients. I'm sure that sunshine-charged raw chocolate is the finest chocolate in the world.

MAKES 16 TRUFFLES

EQUIPMENT
- **bain-marie or dehydrator**
- **stainless-steel hand whisk**
- **16-hole silicone chocolate mould**

INGREDIENTS
- **60 g/2¼ oz raw cacao butter**
- **2 tbsp raw almond butter**
- **3 tbsp raw cacao powder**
- **1 tbsp lucuma powder**
- **85 g/3 oz yacon syrup**
- **10 drops vanilla essential oil**

1 Put the cacao butter in a glass mixing bowl and leave to melt naturally in the sun, or melt gently in a bain-marie or dehydrator (*see* pages 20–1).

2 Add all the other ingredients to the bowl on top of the melted cacao butter. Use the hand whisk to gently stir your ingredients lovingly together – no need to do any fast, frenzied whisking!

3 Spoon the runny chocolate into the holes of the mould so that it fills each one to the very top.

4 Bang the tray firmly on the work surface to help any air bubbles rise to the top and then place in the freezer for about 30 minutes or, if you are travelling, in an alternative, very cool place until the chocolate has firmly set.

5 Retrieve your mould, tip it upside down onto a chopping board and pop the truffles out one by one. If there are any truffles that aren't eaten immediately, store them in an airtight glass jar in the refrigerator for up to 3–4 weeks.

Jessica's nutritional tip
Almonds are a great source of protein, dietary fibre, calcium, vitamin E, niacin and riboflavin. They can be eaten raw, soaked, sprouted, or dehydrated or made into flour, milk or butter.

Raw Chocolate Cheesecake

This has a nice, crunchy-textured base to it, a classic creamy cheesecake filling (but without the usual animal by-products) and a crisp layer of icing spread over the top. It's a very easy cake to make, which is a definite added bonus.

MAKES ONE 20-CM/8-INCH SQUARE CAKE

EQUIPMENT
- **bain-marie or dehydrator**
- **power blender**
- **20-cm/8-inch square silicone cake mould**
- **stainless-steel hand whisk**

INGREDIENTS

Base
- **100 g/3½ oz raw cacao butter**
- **75 g/2¾ oz raw cashew nuts**
- **3 tbsp xylitol crystals**
- **5–6 drops vanilla essential oil or 2 vanilla pods, split lengthways and seeds scraped out**
- **2 tbsp lucuma powder**
- **150 g/5½ oz raisins**
- **100 g/3½ oz Buckwheaties (see page 22)**

Chocolate layer
- **125 g/4½ oz raw Brazil nuts**
- **1 avocado, stoned and peeled**
- **5 tbsp raw cacao powder**
- **5 tbsp raw coconut oil**
- **5 tbsp lucuma powder**
- **85 g/3 oz yacon syrup**
- **pinch of pink crystal salt**

Frosting
- **50 g/1¾ oz raw cacao butter**
- **2 tbsp lucuma powder**
- **2 tbsp xylitol crystals**
- **3–4 drops orange essential oil**

1 Melt the cacao butter gently in a bain-marie or dehydrator until runny (*see* pages 20–1).

2 Process the cashew nuts in your power blender on full power, using the plunger, until they form a fine flour. Use a butter knife or chopstick to scrape away the milled nuts from the base and side of the blender jug if they have stuck.

3 Add the melted cacao butter, xylitol crystals, vanilla oil or seeds and lucuma powder to the milled nuts in your blender jug and blend on full power, using the plunger, until all the ingredients are completely broken down.

4 Add the raisins to the blender jug and then process again, using the plunger, until they are thoroughly blended with the other ingredients.

5 Add your Buckwheaties and process for just a few seconds, using the plunger, just enough for them to be dispersed through the mixture but not enough for them to lose their wonderful crunch.

6 Spoon the mixture into the silicone cake mould and smooth with the back of a tablespoon or your fingers until it looks neat and even. Place in the freezer while you prepare the chocolate layer.

7 Process the Brazil nuts in your power blender as you did the cashew nuts. Add all the other ingredients for the chocolate layer to the milled nuts in the blender jug and blend thoroughly, using the plunger, until you have a thick, rich, chocolatey mixture.

8 Remove your cake mould from the freezer and spoon the chocolate mixture on top of the base. Use a butter knife to make sure that it looks nice and smooth. Place back in the freezer for this layer to firm while you make the frosting.

9 Melt the cacao butter in a glass mixing bowl, as before. Add all the other frosting ingredients to the bowl and use the hand whisk in a figure-of-eight motion to whisk together until you achieve a smooth texture.

10 Take your cake out of the freezer and spoon the frosting over the top of the chocolate layer, making sure that the whole cake is thoroughly covered. Return to the freezer for around 15 minutes to set. Store in the refrigerator, covered, for up to 10 days.

Raw Chocolate Brownies

A moist, luscious chocolate brownie is what every great recipe book needs. As I'm all about using raw chocolate as a tool to help you take your health to the next level, I've sought to replicate this classic cake using walnuts and almonds as the base. When combined with antioxidant icing, it makes for a sumptuous, satisfying, wholesome treat. The great thing that sets this brownie recipe apart from the rest is that you don't have to bake or even dehydrate anything. These brownies can be served alongside a raw ice cream as a filling dessert, cut into slightly smaller pieces and served as a sweet canapé or if you just fancy a bite-sized speedy snack straight from the refrigerator.

MAKES 20 MEDIUM-SIZED BROWNIES

EQUIPMENT
- **bain-marie or dehydrator**
- **food processor**
- **power blender**
- **20-cm x 22-cm/8-inch x 8½-inch rectangular silicone cake mould**

INGREDIENTS
- **100 g/3½ oz raw coconut oil**
- **150 g/5½ oz raw whole almonds**
- **50 g/1¾ oz raw cacao powder**
- **400 g/14 oz fresh dates, stoned and chopped widthways into 3 pieces**
- **125 g/4½ oz raw walnut halves**
- **3 heaped tsp xylitol crystals, plus extra for sprinkling**
- **pinch of pink crystal salt**
- **20 g/¾ oz yacon syrup**
- **50 ml/2 fl oz fresh filtered water**

Antioxidant icing
- **60 g/2¼ oz raw cacao butter**
- **75 g/2¾ oz raw cashew nuts**
- **¼ tsp purple corn extract powder (optional)**
- **4 heaped tsp xylitol crystals**
- **90 g/3¼ oz fresh blueberries**

1 If your coconut oil has hardened and turned white, melt it gently in a bain-marie or dehydrator until a clear liquid (*see pages 20–1*).

2 Process the almonds in your food processor until roughly ground.

3 Add the coconut oil, cacao powder, dates, 75 g/2¾ oz of the walnuts, the xylitol crystals and salt to the almonds in the food processor. Process until all ingredients are completely broken down, stopping the food processor to stir the ingredients with a spoon if necessary, just to help it along. You should have a thick, brown mixture when it's done.

4 Spoon the mixture into a large mixing bowl and stir in the remaining walnuts, the yacon syrup and water until it turns sticky.

5 Spoon into the cake mould, making sure that the mixture reaches each side of the mould, including the corners. Use the back of the spoon to smooth the top of the mixture evenly.

6 Place in the freezer for 30 minutes or until firm but not frozen.

7 Meanwhile, make the icing. Melt the cacao butter gently in a bain-marie or dehydrator until runny (*see pages 20–1*).

8 Process the cashew nuts in your power blender on full power, using the plunger, until they form a fine flour. Use a butter knife or chopstick to scrape the milled nuts away from the base and side of the blender jug if they have stuck.

9 Add the melted cacao butter, purple corn extract powder (if using), xylitol crystals and blueberries to the milled nuts in the blender and blend on full power, using the plunger, until smooth.

10 Spoon the icing onto your favourite raw cake and place in the freezer for 15 minutes or until firm and set. The icing can be stored in an airtight glass jar in the refrigerator for up to 3 days.

11 Remove the firm cake from the freezer and add the vibrant purple icing to the top of the cake using a tablespoon. The back of the spoon, a knife or a spatula all work well to smooth it over. I like to create swirls in the thick icing with sweeping actions using the back of a metal tablespoon. I also don't take the icing right to the edge for this recipe but leave a 1-cm/½-inch border around the entire cake for an eye-catching effect.

12 Return the cake to the freezer for 15 minutes or until the icing has set firmly.

13 Take the cake out of the freezer and peel the sides of the mould away from the cake to loosen it slightly. While the cake is still quite firm from being in the freezer, lift it straight out onto a chopping board and sprinkle lightly with xylitol crystals to decorate. Slice into roughly 4-cm/1½-inch squares and either serve immediately or keep it refrigerated, covered, for up to 3 days.

Rich Raw Chocolate + Vanilla Torte

This is one of those cakes that is suitable for all occasions, be it birthdays, Christmas festivities, summer beach parties, a house warming party or just because you feel like making a super-nutritious cake. Who needs an excuse for making a raw chocolate cake anyway?

MAKES ONE 20-CM/8-INCH ROUND CAKE

EQUIPMENT
- food processor
- bain-marie or dehydrator
- power blender
- 20-cm/8-inch round springform cake tin

INGREDIENTS

Base
- 50 g/1¾ oz raw cashew nuts
- 60 g/2¼ oz raw almonds
- 60 g/2¼ oz raw walnuts
- 2 pinches of ground cinnamon
- 30 g/1 oz raw pumpkin seeds
- 85 g/3 oz ready-to-eat unsulphured dried apricots, chopped
- 1 heaped tsp xylitol crystals
- 10 g/¼ oz Buckwheaties (*see* page 22)
- yacon syrup, for sticking the lining paper

Filling
- 150 g/5½ oz raw cacao butter
- 100 g/3½ oz raw hulled hemp seeds
- 100 g/3½ oz raw cashew nuts
- 1 avocado, stoned and peeled
- 5 tbsp raw cacao powder
- 5 tbsp xylitol crystals
- pinch of pink crystal salt

Vanilla layer
- 75 g/2¾ oz raw coconut oil
- 50 g/1¾ oz raw cashew nuts
- 6 drops vanilla essential oil
- 25 g/1 oz raw agave nectar

Cashew nut cream
- 2 tbsp raw coconut oil
- 75 g/2¾ oz raw cashew nuts
- 3 tbsp xylitol crystals
- 3 drops vanilla essential oil
- 5 tbsp freshly filtered water
- pinch of pink crystal salt

1 To make the base, process all the nuts with the cinnamon in your food processor until they are roughly ground.

2 Add all the other ingredients for the base to the ground nuts in the food processor and process until a soft mixture forms.

3 Place your cake tin on a sheet of greaseproof paper and, using a pencil, draw around the base of the tin. Cut the paper circle out and stick to the bottom of the tin with a few small blobs of yacon syrup.

4 Spoon the mixture for the base on top of the paper and use the back of the spoon or your fingers to press it down firmly and evenly to the edge of the tin. Cover with foil and place in the refrigerator while you prepare the filling.

5 Melt the cacao butter gently in a bain-marie or dehydrator until runny (*see* pages 20–1).

6 Add the hemp seeds and cashew nuts to your power blender and blend on full power, using the plunger, until they form a fine flour. Use a butter knife or chopstick to scrape away the milled seeds and nuts from the base and side of the blender jug if they have stuck.

7 Add the melted cacao butter and all the other filling ingredients to the milled nuts in the blender jug and blend on full power, using the plunger, until you have a smooth, even consistency. The mixture will start to look oily, but this is perfectly normal.

8 Retrieve the cake base from the refrigerator, spoon the filling onto the base and smooth it evenly over using the back of the spoon or a butter knife. Return the cake to the refrigerator, covered in foil, while you make the vanilla layer.

9 If your coconut oil has hardened and turned white, melt it gently in a bain-marie or dehydrator until soft (*see* pages 20–1).

10 Clean and dry your blender jug and plunger. Add the cashew nuts and blend to a fine flour, as in Step 6.

11 Add the coconut oil and all the remaining ingredients to the milled nuts in the blender jug and blend on full power, using the plunger, until you have a smooth, creamy consistency. Take your cake from the refrigerator and pour the vanilla mixture over the top. Use the back of a tablespoon or a butter knife to spread the mixture evenly over the top and to the side of the tin.

12 Re-cover with foil and return to the refrigerator for at least 2 hours until all the layers are firm.

13 Meanwhile, to make the Cashew Nut Cream, if your coconut oil has hardened and turned white, melt it gently in a bain-marie or dehydrator until a clear liquid (*see* pages 20–1). Process the cashew nuts in your power blender using the plunger to a fine powder. Use a butter knife or chopstick to scrape the milled nuts away from the base and side of the blender jug if they have stuck.

14 Add all the other ingredients to your blender jug and blend on full speed using the plunger until you get a smooth, creamy texture. Pour into a small jug.

15 When you are sure that the cake is solid, run a sharp knife around the edge and slowly release the tin. Slice your cake into equal portions and enjoy drizzled with Cashew Nut Cream. Store in an airtight BPA-free plastic container in the refrigerator for up to a week.

Chocolate Goji Finger Biscuits

These biscuits are a great on-the-go snack that will satisfy your sweet-tooth cravings wherever you are. Goji berries are wonderful little fruits, packed with nutrients that will help to fully sustain you.

MAKES 10–12 BISCUITS

EQUIPMENT

- **bain-marie or dehydrator**
- **stainless-steel hand whisk**
- **shallow, medium-sized BPA-free plastic container**

INGREDIENTS

- **70 g/2½ oz raw cacao butter**
- **2 tbsp raw coconut oil**
- **75 g/2¾ oz lucuma powder**
- **2 vanilla pods, split in half lengthways and seeds scraped out**
- **pinch of pink crystal salt**
- **2 tbsp raw cacao powder**
- **75 g/2¾ oz Buckwheaties (see page 22)**
- **25 g/1 oz dried goji berries**
- **2 tbsp raw hulled hemp seeds**
- **16 fresh dates, stoned and chopped widthways into 4 pieces**

1 Melt the cacao butter gently, together with the coconut oil if it has hardened and turned white, in a bain-marie or dehydrator until runny (*see pages 20–1*).

2 Add the melted cacao butter and coconut oil, lucuma powder, vanilla seeds, salt and cacao powder to a large mixing bowl. Mix together thoroughly with the hand whisk.

3 Stir in the Buckwheaties, goji berries, hemp seeds and dates with a spoon.

4 Spoon the mixture into a medium-sized BPA-free plastic container about 2.5 cm/1 inch deep. Shake the container from side to side a few times and then bang the base firmly down on your work surface to help any air bubbles rise to the top. Place in your freezer for 30 minutes or until solid.

5 Tip the container upside down onto a chopping board to release your chocolate and then use a very sharp knife to cut it into finger-sized pieces. Store in an airtight glass jar in the refrigerator for up to a month.

Jessica's nutritional tip

Goji berries are particularly high in vitamins B1, B2 and B6, which can help counter the depletion of our B-vitamin stores which is one of the effects of suffering from stress.

White Chocolate + Raisin Snaps

Providing you've got some Buckwheaties ready made, you can make a jar of your very own biscuits in under 30 minutes, and without the hassle of using the oven. I love the way that eating healthily can also be quick and easy.

MAKES 16 SNAPS

EQUIPMENT
• **bain-marie or dehydrator**
• **power blender**

INGREDIENTS
• **100 g/3½ oz raw cacao butter**
• **75 g/2¾ oz raw cashew nuts**
• **3 tbsp xylitol crystals**
• **5–6 drops vanilla essential oil or 3 vanilla pods, split lengthways and seeds scraped out**
• **2 tbsp lucuma powder**
• **150 g/5½ oz raisins**
• **100 g/3½ oz Buckwheaties (see page 22)**

1 Melt the cacao butter gently in a bain-marie or dehydrator until runny (*see pages 20–1*).

2 Process the cashew nuts in your blender on full power, using the plunger, until they form a fine flour. Use a butter knife or chopstick to scrape the milled nuts away from the base and side of the blender jug if they have stuck.

3 Add the melted cacao butter to the milled nuts in the blender jug with the xylitol crystals, vanilla oil or seeds and lucuma powder. Blend on full power, using the plunger, until smooth.

4 Mix the raisins and Buckwheaties together on a baking tray. Spoon the runny white chocolate over the raisins and Buckwheaties and stir thoroughly with a metal tablespoon until evenly coated. Use the back of the spoon to press the mixture down over the base of the tray in a sweeping movement until it forms an even layer about 1 cm/½ inch deep.

5 Place in your freezer for around 20 minutes or until the chocolate has properly set around the raisins and Buckwheaties.

6 Take the baking tray out of the freezer and tip it upside down onto a chopping board. Gently bang down until the heavy block of white chocolate biscuit falls out with a thud. Use a very sharp knife to cut the block into rectangular-shaped pieces. Store in an airtight glass jar in the refrigerator for up to a month, if they are not all eaten up straight away!

Raw Chocolate Gingerbread People

These cute little gingerbread people aren't too rich, so they're perfect for little tummies – and bigger ones too of course. Although I wouldn't advise children under the age of three to eat any type of chocolate, whether raw or roasted, if you have an older child who is used to conventional chocolate and you are looking for a healthy alternative treat, this is a sound option. These also travel pretty well in an airtight food container.

MAKES 27 SMALL GINGERBREAD PEOPLE

EQUIPMENT
- **food processor**
- **gingerbread people biscuit cutters**
- **dehydrator with mesh screen**

INGREDIENTS
- **250 g/9 oz raw pecan nuts**
- **300 g/10½ oz fresh dates, stoned and halved widthways**
- **6 drops ginger essential oil**
- **1 tbsp raw cacao powder**
- **2 tsp xylitol crystals**
- **50 ml/2 fl oz raw almond milk, preferably unsweetened (see Raw Nut and Seed Milk, page 23)**
- **pinch of pink crystal salt**
- **lucuma powder, for sprinkling**
- **54 dried goji berries**
- **54 small raisins**

Jessica's top tip
This recipe works well without the raw cacao powder, so if you want to make these gingerbread people for younger children, just omit this ingredient – and the ginger essential oil too if you wish.

1 Process the pecan nuts in your food processor until roughly ground.

2 Add the dates, ginger essential oil, cacao powder, xylitol crystals, almond milk and salt to the ground nuts in the food processor and process until the mixture clumps together to form a dough. This may take a few minutes.

3 Sprinkle a wooden chopping board and rolling pin lightly with lucuma powder to prevent sticking. Place the lump of dough on top of the lucuma powder before rolling out to a thickness of 5 mm–1 cm/¼–½ inch.

4 Using the biscuit cutters, cut out gingerbread people from the dough and place them on the mesh screen, lining them up closely together but without actually touching. Keep re-rolling the dough and cutting out the gingerbread people until the dough is all used up.

5 Add 2 goji berries for buttons and 2 raisins for eyes to each gingerbread character, pressing them in firmly. Place the mesh screen in your dehydrator and dehydrate at 40.5°C/105°F for 18 hours or until firm. Store in a BPA-free plastic container for up to a week.

Love Macaroons

This recipe will provide you with an ample supply of chunky, raw chocolate-flavoured macaroon-style cakes. As you will need a dehydrator for this recipe and it takes time for them to dehydrate, I like to make up a big batch to make it worth my while. But if you don't want so many, feel free to simply halve the quantities.

MAKES 8 MACAROONS

EQUIPMENT
- **food processor**
- **two 8-hole heart-shaped silicone cake moulds**
- **dehydrator with mesh screen**
- **bain-marie or dehydrator**
- **power blender**

INGREDIENTS
Macaroons
- **150 g/5½ oz raw pecan nuts**
- **50 g/1¾ oz raw almonds**
- **pinch of pink crystal salt**
- **150 g/5½ oz fresh dates, stoned and halved widthways**
- **2 tbsp raw cacao powder**
- **¼ tsp ground cinnamon**
- **50 ml/2 fl oz fresh filtered water**

Filling
- **40 g/1½ oz raw cacao butter**
- **1 tbsp raw coconut oil**
- **70 g/2½ oz stoned, peeled avocado**
- **2 tbsp xylitol crystals**
- **5 drops vanilla essential oil**
- **2 heaped tbsp raw cacao powder**
- **1 heaped tbsp lucuma powder**

1 Process the pecan nuts and almonds with the salt in your food processor until roughly ground.

2 Add all the other ingredients for the macaroons, except the water, to the ground nuts in the food processor and begin to process. While the machine is running, slowly add the water through the chute. Process until a sticky mixture forms.

3 Spoon the mixture into each hole of the heart-shaped cake moulds until no more than 1 cm/½ inch in depth. Press down with the back of the spoon or your fingers to flatten to the edges.

4 Place the moulds on a mesh screen in your dehydrator and dehydrate at 40.5°C/105°F for 1 hour. After this time the heart shapes should be a little more solid so that you can carefully pop them out of the moulds, while maintaining their beautiful shape, directly onto the screen. Dehydrate for a further 3 hours.

5 When the hearts are almost ready to retrieve from your dehydrator, melt the cacao butter gently, together with the coconut oil if it has hardened and turned white, in a bain-marie or dehydrator until runny (see pages 20–1).

6 Add the melted cacao butter and coconut oil with all the remaining ingredients to your power blender jug and blend on high power, using the plunger, until you have a smooth, creamy paste.

7 Remove the macaroons from the dehydrator and top 8 of the hearts with about 4 teaspoonfuls of the filling. Sandwich the remaining 8 hearts on top and press down gently until the filling starts to seep out of the sides. Enjoy straight away while still warm. The macaroons can be stored in an airtight BPA-free plastic container in the refrigerator for up to a week, although the filling will harden once they have been refrigerated.

Neapolitan Ice Cream

Neapolitan ice cream usually consists of vanilla, strawberry and chocolate-flavoured ice cream, but in this raw food version I have used cherry ice cream instead of strawberry because I love the lively taste of frozen cherries. However, if you want to stick with tradition, just substitute the cherries for strawberries and prepare the ice cream in exactly the same way. The minty raw chocolate topping is specially designed to be poured over individual servings of the ice cream (the quantity given serves two) and returned to the freezer, where it will magically set hard after just a few minutes.

SERVES 12

EQUIPMENT
- power blender
- 20-cm/8-inch square silicone cake mould or BPA-free plastic container
- bain-marie or dehydrator
- stainless-steel hand whisk

INGREDIENTS

Vanilla ice cream
- 150 g/5½ oz raw cashew nuts
- 6 drops vanilla essential oil
- 150 ml/5 fl oz fresh filtered water
- 85 g/3 oz raw agave nectar

Cherry ice cream
- 150 g/5½ oz raw cashew nuts
- 100 ml/3½ fl oz fresh filtered water
- 150 g/5½ oz frozen or fresh cherries, stoned
- 50 g/1¾ oz raw agave nectar

Chocolate ice cream
- 150 g/5½ oz raw cashew nuts
- 3 tbsp raw cacao powder
- 150 ml/5 fl oz fresh filtered water
- 50 g/1¾ oz raw agave nectar

Mint chocolate topping
(enough for 2 ice cream servings)
- 60 g/2½ oz raw coconut oil
- 2½ tbsp raw cacao powder
- 1 tbsp xylitol crystals
- 3 drops peppermint essential oil
- 1 tbsp yacon syrup

1 For the vanilla ice cream, add the cashew nuts to your blender and blend on full power, using the plunger, until they form a fine flour. Use a butter knife or chopstick to scrape away the milled nuts from the base and side of the blender jug if they have stuck.

2 Add all the other ingredients for the vanilla ice cream to the milled nuts in the blender jug and blend on full power, using the plunger, until smooth and creamy. Spoon the mixture into your mould and smooth over with the back of the spoon before placing it, uncovered, in the freezer.

3 Clean and dry your blender and plunger. Repeat Step 1 with the ingredients for the cherry ice cream, but pour the mixture into a glass dish and place it, covered with foil, in the refrigerator.

4 Clean and dry your blender and plunger, then repeat Step 1 once more with the ingredients for the chocolate ice cream. Pour it into a separate glass dish, cover and place in the refrigerator.

5 When the vanilla ice cream has set firmly, usually after about 3–4 hours, take the cherry ice cream mixture out of your refrigerator and spoon it carefully over the top of the vanilla, taking care not to drip any down the inside of the mould. If you do, just wipe it away with kitchen paper, then return to the freezer to harden.

6 When the cherry ice cream layer has set firmly after a similar amount of time, add the chocolate ice cream mixture and smooth it over the cherry layer, as in Step 5. Place back in the freezer, covered with foil, for 8 hours, or preferably overnight, for the layers to fully set.

7 Once the ice cream is set, make the topping. If your coconut oil has hardened and turned white, melt it gently in a bain-marie or dehydrator until a clear liquid (*see pages 20–1*).

8 Place the coconut oil with all the other topping ingredients in a medium-sized mixing bowl. Using the hand whisk, whisk together thoroughly until a creamy, runny, chocolatey consistency begins to emerge.

9 Remove the mould from the freezer. Turn upside down onto a chopping board and let the block of striped ice cream fall out. Slice off 2 portions, admiring the pretty, stripy layers that you've created, and place in serving dishes. Pour the topping over the ice cream and return to the freezer for 10 minutes or until the topping is firmly set.

10 Store the remainder of the ice cream in an airtight BPA-free plastic container in your freezer for up to a week, although the flavour may become slightly more subtle as time goes by.

Jessica's top tip
The mint chocolate topping can be used for any other raw ice cream or dessert dish.

Summer Sorbet

This refreshing sorbet can be eaten at any time, but it's best enjoyed in the garden on a hot summer's day. I used to serve this sorbet in shot glasses as an amuse-bouche at my monthly five-course raw food dinner parties.

SERVES 6

EQUIPMENT
- power blender
- six 50-ml/2-fl oz shot glasses

INGREDIENTS
- 150 g/5½ oz peeled and deseeded cantaloupe melon
- 3 tbsp freshly squeezed lemon juice
- 60 g/2¼ oz raw agave nectar
- 18 fresh or frozen raspberries
- 3 tsp raw cacao nibs

1 Add the melon, lemon juice and agave nectar to your power blender jug and blend on full power until smooth.

2 Divide the mixture evenly between the 6 shot glasses. Add 3 raspberries to each glass, then ½ teaspoon cacao nibs sprinkled on top. Place, uncovered, in the freezer for at least 6 hours or until frozen. The sorbets can be stored in the freezer for up to a month, although the fresher the better.

Beetroot + Mint Choc Chip Sorbet

The colour of this sorbet delights me, as it looks so vibrant. This makes an incredibly refreshing, tantalizing and palate-cleansing treat, but whatever you do, just don't spill it on the carpet!

SERVES 4

EQUIPMENT
- power blender
- four 50-ml/2-fl oz shot glasses

INGREDIENTS
- 85 g/3 oz peeled beetroot
- 6 tbsp freshly squeezed orange juice
- 90 g/3¼ oz raw agave nectar
- 4 drops peppermint essential oil
- 2 tsp raw cacao nibs

1 Add all the ingredients, except the cacao nibs, to your power blender jug and blend on full power until smooth.

2 Add ½ teaspoon cacao nibs to the bottom of each of the 4 shot glasses, then pour the mixture from your blender over the top. Place, uncovered, in the freezer for 8 hours or overnight until frozen. The sorbets can be stored in the freezer for up to a month, although I recommend enjoying them before this time as the flavour and colour may start to fade.

Jessica's top tip
Be very careful when freezing glasses. Make sure they're uncovered so that the liquid can expand when it freezes, and store them in such a way that there's no danger of breakage.

Guarana + Goji Nutty Loaf

A slightly sweet, dense, intensely nutty cake that doesn't need baking – this is another example of how raw food makes life much easier for you. The loaf also travels well, making it an ideal snack if you're on the move.

MAKES TWO 20-CM X 8-CM/
8-INCH X 4-INCH LOAVES

EQUIPMENT
- **bain-marie or dehydrator**
- **food processor**
- **two 20-cm x 8-cm/8-inch x 4-inch silicone cake moulds (designed for bread-making)**
- **power blender**

INGREDIENTS
- **60 g/2¼ oz raw coconut oil**
- **100 g/3½ oz raw sunflower seeds**
- **250 g/9 oz raw walnut halves**
- **5 tbsp raw cacao powder**
- **300 g/10½ oz fresh dates, stoned and chopped widthways into 3 pieces**
- **2 heaped tsp lucuma powder**
- **1 tsp pure guarana powder**
- **2 tbsp raw agave nectar**
- **pinch of pink crystal salt**

Chocolate icing
40 g/1½ oz raw cacao butter
1 tbsp raw coconut oil
50 g/1¾ oz raw hulled hemp seeds
3 tbsp raw cacao powder
4 tbsp raw agave nectar

To decorate
1 handful dried goji berries
½ tsp xylitol crystals

1 If your coconut oil has hardened and turned white, melt it gently in a bain-marie or dehydrator until a clear liquid (*see pages 20–1*).

2 Process the sunflower seeds in your food processor until they turn into rough flour, without any whole seeds remaining.

3 Add the coconut oil, walnuts, cacao powder, dates, lucuma powder, guarana powder, agave nectar and salt to the milled seeds in your food processor and process until all the ingredients are broken down. You may need to stop the food processor and stir the ingredients with a metal spoon to help it to process them efficiently.

4 Divide the mixture between the cake moulds and smooth over the tops with the back of a metal tablespoon, ensuring that the mixture reaches the edges and corners of the moulds. Place in the freezer for 30 minutes or until firm.

5 To make the icing, melt the cacao butter and coconut oil gently in a bain-marie or dehydrator as before. Process the hemp seeds in your power blender on full power, using the plunger, until they form a fine flour. Use a butter knife or chopstick to scrape the milled seeds away from the base and side of the blender jug if they have stuck.

6 Pour the melted cacao butter and coconut oil over the milled hemp seeds in the blender jug and add the cacao powder and agave nectar. Blend on full power, using the plunger, until you have a smooth consistency.

7 When the loaves are nice and firm, take them from the freezer and spoon the icing directly from your power blender evenly onto both loaves. Use the back of the spoon to make sure that the icing reaches all four sides of each mould and is as even as possible.

8 Sprinkle the loaves with the goji berries and xylitol crystals to decorate and return to the freezer for 15 minutes or until the icing has hardened.

9 Retrieve your loaf moulds from the freezer and gently pull the sides of each mould away from the loaves. While the loaves are still hard from being in the freezer, lift them out one at a time from the moulds directly onto a large chopping board. Using a very sharp knife, cut the loaves widthways into 2.5-cm/1-inch thick slices and serve. Store in the refrigerator, covered, for up to 10 days.

Little Leo's Pudding

This is my young son Leo's current favourite recipe. He enjoys a mostly raw, vegan diet on which he continues to flourish. I'm always designing new recipes that are nutrient rich for him, as it's my goal to fill him up on calories that are loaded with goodness to fuel his rapid growth and exceed his daily requirements. Little Leo's Pudding was originally invented without cacao since he was under three years old, but one day I sampled the leftovers sprinkled with raw cacao nibs and discovered how good it tasted. This recipe is very versatile: you can remove the cacao nibs to make it a non-chocolate recipe depending on what you fancy and whether you are making it for a young child. It makes a wholesome dessert to finish off a raw food main course.

SERVES 2

EQUIPMENT
- **bain-marie or dehydrator**
- **power blender**

INGREDIENTS
- **1 avocado**
- **3 tbsp raw hulled hemp seeds**
- **1 tbsp xylitol crystals**
- **1 tbsp lucuma powder**
- **1 heaped tbsp raw coconut oil**
- **2 handfuls dried goji berries**
- **1 banana, peeled**
- **1 tbsp raw cacao nibs**
- **1 tbsp Pink Buckwheaties (*see page 22*)**

1 If your coconut oil has hardened and turned white, melt it gently in a bain-marie or dehydrator until soft or runny (*see pages 20–1*).

2 Add the coconut oil with all the other ingredients, except the cacao nibs, to your power blender jug and blend on full power, using the plunger, until smooth.

3 Spoon into 2 bowls and sprinkle with the cacao nibs and Pink Buckwheaties. The pudding will keep in an airtight BPA-free plastic container in the refrigerator for up to 24 hours.

White Raw Choc Chip Pudding

This is a lovely quick and easy dessert if you feel like something rich and fulfilling, but don't want to experience a typical chocolatey flavour. I like making this as a dessert for the solstice celebrations as it's rich and creamy and incredibly enjoyable to eat with others.

SERVES 1

EQUIPMENT
- **bain-marie or dehydrator**
- **power blender**

INGREDIENTS
- **50 g/1¾ oz raw cacao butter**
- **1 tbsp raw coconut oil**
- **100 g/3½ oz raw cashew nuts**
- **3 tbsp xylitol crystals**
- **3 drops vanilla essential oil**
- **pinch of pink crystal salt**
- **20 g/¾ oz raw cacao nibs**
- **25 g/1 oz yacon syrup**

1 Melt the cacao butter gently, together with the coconut oil if it has hardened and turned white, in a bain-marie or dehydrator until runny (*see pages 20–1*).

2 Process the cashew nuts in your power blender on full power, using the plunger, until they form a fine flour. Use a butter knife or chopstick to scrape the milled nuts away from the base and side of the blender jug if they have stuck.

3 Add the cacao butter and all the other ingredients to your power blender jug and blend thoroughly on full power, using the plunger, until creamy.

4 Serve immediately in a small glass to enjoy it in its soft state, or place in the freezer for about 30 minutes for a firmer dessert. Store in the refrigerator, covered, for up to 3 days.

Tingly Raw Chocolate Body Paint

This fresh and tingly raw chocolate body paint will not only provide you and your partner with hours of fun as a more unusual type of dessert but can also heighten your intimate experience. The emperor Montezuma claimed to drink up to 50 cups of dark chocolate over a day for its qualities as an aphrodisiac. So go on and give this potent dessert a try.

MAKES 90 G/3¼ OZ

EQUIPMENT
- **bain-marie**
- **stainless-steel hand whisk**

INGREDIENTS
- **40 g/1½ oz raw cacao butter**
- **3 tbsp raw cacao powder**
- **35 g/1¼ oz raw agave nectar**
- **4 drops peppermint essential oil**

1 Melt the cacao butter gently in a bain-marie or dehydrator until runny (*see pages 20–1*).

2 When the cacao butter has fully melted, spoon in the cacao powder before pouring in the agave nectar and adding the peppermint essential oil. Using the hand whisk, gently whisk the mixture until the powder and liquids are fully combined.

3 Take the glass mixing bowl out of the pan of hot water and use before the butter sets.

Jessica's top tip
Your body temperature regulates at around 37°C/98°F, which is very similar to the melting point of raw cacao butter. This makes it the perfect sensual, melt-in-the-mouth aphrodisiac.

Raw Hemp + Chocolate Spread

If your kids eat conventional chocolate spread and you want to get them eating food that isn't going to jeopardize their health in the long term, then this is probably the most nutritious chocolate spread available. And by creating your own spread at home with your child, you are also keeping the cost down and making them feel involved at the same time. The flax seed oil and hemp seeds are fantastic for omega-3, -6 and -9 essential fatty acids, which are vital for healthy brain growth.

MAKES 350 G/12 OZ

EQUIPMENT

- **bain-marie or dehydrator**
- **power blender**
- **medium-sized airtight glass jar**

INGREDIENTS

- **100 g/3½ oz raw coconut oil**
- **150 g/5½ raw hulled hemp seeds**
- **75 ml/2½ fl oz cold-pressed flax seed oil**
- **100 g/3½ oz raw agave nectar**
- **3 tbsp raw cacao powder**
- **pinch of pink crystal salt**

1 If the coconut oil is too firm to blend, melt it down gently into a soft consistency in a bain-marie or dehydrator (*see* pages 20–1).

2 Process the hemp seeds in your power blender on full power, using the plunger, until they form a fine flour. Use a butter knife or chopstick to scrape the milled seeds away from the base and side of the blender jug if they have stuck.

3 Add the coconut oil and all the other ingredients to the milled seeds in your power blender jug and blend on full power, using the plunger, until smooth and runny.

4 Pour into the glass jar and add the lid. Place in the refrigerator until firm yet spreadable. Due to the inclusion of the flax seed oil, you should be able to spread it once it has set. Store in the jar in the refrigerator for up to a month.

Jessica's top tip
Spread onto slices of freshly peeled banana for moreish, energy-enhancing canapés.

Raw Chocolate Jellies

These are great for children's birthday parties – and adults' too. It looks and tastes like proper jelly yet it doesn't contain gelatine, which is an animal by-product, as I prefer to use agar – a sea vegetable containing a wide array of minerals. Although agar is not strictly a raw food, I still include it in my diet because of its outstanding mineral count. Just make sure that you cool the bowl of agar thoroughly to ensure that it doesn't heat the raw cacao powder and lead to it losing its wonderful health-boosting properties. My version of single cream to accompany the jelly is rich and creamy despite being non-dairy.

SERVES 2 ADULTS OR 3 CHILDREN

EQUIPMENT
- **saucepan**
- **8-hole (4-cm/1½-inch diameter) silicone jelly, chocolate or cake mould**
- **bain-marie or dehydrator**
- **power blender**

INGREDIENTS
- **250 ml/9 fl oz fresh filtered water**
- **1½ tbsp agar flakes**
- **1 tbsp raw cacao powder**
- **1 tbsp xylitol crystals**

Cashew nut cream
- **2 tbsp raw coconut oil**
- **75 g/2¾ oz raw cashew nuts**
- **3 tbsp xylitol crystals**
- **3 drops vanilla essential oil**
- **5 tbsp fresh filtered water**
- **pinch of pink crystal salt**

Jessica's nutritional tip
Agar is rich in trace minerals and iodine. Iodine helps to make thyroid hormones, which play an important role in maintaining the body's metabolic rate and cells.

1 Add the water to a saucepan and sprinkle the agar flakes on top, without stirring. Bring the pan to a simmer and stir occasionally. Keep simmering for up to 3 minutes or until the flakes are fully dissolved. Pour the mixture into a glass mixing bowl and leave to cool for about 15–20 minutes.

2 When the agar mixture is warm rather than hot, add the cacao powder and xylitol crystals and gently stir with a spoon until fully dissolved. Pour into the holes of your silicone mould, cover with foil and place on an even surface in the refrigerator for 30 minutes or until firm.

3 Meanwhile, to make the cream, if your coconut oil has hardened and turned white, melt it gently in a bain-marie or dehydrator until a clear liquid (*see* pages 20–1).

4 Process the cashew nuts in your power blender on full power, using the plunger, until they form a fine flour. Use a butter knife or chopstick to scrape the milled nuts away from the base and side of the blender jug if they have stuck.

5 Add the coconut oil and all the other ingredients to the milled nuts in the blender jug and blend on full power, using the plunger, until you have a smooth, creamy texture. Pour into a small jug and keep refrigerated, covered, until ready to serve (up to 48 hours).

6 Retrieve your mould from the refrigerator when set and invert to release the jellies directly onto a serving platter. Serve with the cream. The jellies can be stored in the refrigerator, covered, for up to 3 days

Crêpes

Considered to be a national dish in France, crêpes are now widely consumed. They are traditionally made from wheat flour and then fried, but here I have created raw crêpes from flax seed flour, which is far better for your health than wheat flour. These crêpes also have bananas added to the batter, which will sustain you and leave you feeling energized and satisfied.

MAKES 3 LARGE CRÊPES

EQUIPMENT

- **power blender**
- **food processor**
- **bain-marie**
- **dehydrator with 3 solid dehydrator sheets and 3 mesh screens**
- **stainless-steel hand whisk**

INGREDIENTS

- **250 g/9 oz flax seeds**
- **5 bananas, peeled and quartered**
- **½ tsp mixed spice**
- **1 tsp xylitol crystals**
- **150 ml/5 fl oz fresh filtered water**
- **pinch of pink crystal salt**

Chocolicious sauce
- **100 g/3½ oz raw cacao butter**
- **6 tbsp raw cacao powder**
- **85 g/3 oz raw agave nectar**

To serve
- **your favourite prepared fresh fruits, such as strawberries, bananas and blueberries**

Jessica's nutritional tip
Roughly 50 per cent more omega-3 fatty acid can be found in flax seeds and flax seed oil than you would get from fish oils.

1 Process the flax seeds in your power blender on full power, using the plunger, until they form a fine flour. Use a butter knife or chopstick to scrape the milled seeds away from the base and side of the blender jug if they have stuck.

2 Add the milled seeds to your food processor along with all the other ingredients and process on full power, using the plunger, until a thick, smooth batter forms. You may need to stop your machine for a moment and stir the ingredients with a spoon.

3 Divide the batter into thirds and spoon one third onto each solid dehydrator sheet. Use a spatula to help spread each amount of mixture into a circle no more than 5 mm/¼ inch deep and smooth the surface.

4 Place the sheets in your dehydrator and dehydrate at 40.5°C/105°F for 4 hours. Remove the sheets, tip each crêpe onto a mesh screen and slowly peel back each sheet, leaving the crêpes sticky side up. Place the mesh screens in your dehydrator and dehydrate for a further 4 hours or until the crêpes are not at all sticky but completely flexible.

5 Meanwhile, make the Chocolicious Sauce. Melt the cacao butter in a bain-marie or dehydrator until runny (*see pages 20–1*).

6 When the cacao butter has fully melted, spoon in the cacao powder before pouring in the agave nectar. Using the hand whisk, gently whisk the mixture until the powder and liquids are fully combined.

7 Place each crêpe on a plate, top with your favourite fresh fruits and roll up to enclose. Pour over the warm Chocolicious Sauce to cover. Enjoy straight away. The unfilled crêpes will keep in a cool, dry place, covered in foil, for up to a week.

Banana Split

The famous banana split has just turned raw and incredibly nutritious! I've been making healthy recipes for so long now that I actually wouldn't know what to do if I was given the task of making something that contained refined sugar and other unhealthy ingredients. I relish the challenge of making healthier versions of everyone's 'naughty but nice' dishes, and a banana split has got to be one of my childhood favourites. The caramel sauce owes its unique, full-bodied flavour to the presence of the yacon syrup, and also works well drizzled over raw chocolate cake.

SERVES 2

EQUIPMENT
- **power blender**
- **small BPA-free plastic container**
- **stainless-steel hand whisk**
- **ice cream scoop (optional)**

INGREDIENTS

Chocolate ice cream
- **150 g/5½ oz raw cashew nuts**
- **3 tbsp raw cacao powder**
- **150 ml/5 fl oz fresh filtered water**
- **50 g/1¾ oz raw agave nectar**

Yacon caramel sauce
- **4 tbsp yacon syrup**
- **2 tbsp xylitol crystals**
- **4 drops vanilla essential oil**
- **1 tbsp lucuma powder**

To serve
- **2 large bananas**
- **8 raspberries**

Jessica's top tip
I recommend adding Chocolicious Sauce (*see* page 82) over the split instead of, or as well as, the caramel sauce.

1 Process the cashew nuts in your power blender on full power, using the plunger, until they form a fine flour. Use a butter knife or chopstick to scrape the milled nuts away from the base and side of the blender jug if they have stuck.

2 Add all the other ingredients for the chocolate ice cream to the milled nuts in your blender jug and blend on full power, using the plunger, until smooth and creamy. Pour into the BPA-free plastic container and place in the freezer, uncovered, for about 3–4 hours until completely frozen.

3 When the ice cream has frozen, make the sauce. Add all the ingredients to a small mixing bowl and whisk thoroughly with the hand whisk until you have a runny sauce texture.

4 Peel the bananas, place each one in a bowl and slice lengthways down the centre with a sharp knife, allowing it to fall open. Divide the chocolate ice cream between the 2 bowls, either using a metal spoon dipped in warm water to help it glide through or a proper ice cream scoop to achieve a portion of beautifully presented ice cream. Add 4 raspberries to each bowl, then pour the sauce over the ice cream and fresh banana. Enjoy straight away with someone you love. Any leftover sauce can be stored in an airtight glass jar in the refrigerator for up to a week.

Birthday Cake

This birthday cake recipe with its contrasting light, sweet vanilla cream centre, finished with a drizzle of white chocolate peppermint icing, is suitable for anyone over the age of three years.

SERVES 16 SMALL SLICES

EQUIPMENT
- bain-marie or dehydrator
- food processor
- power blender
- stainless-steel hand whisk
- 25-cm/10-inch spring form cake tin

INGREDIENTS

Base
- 2 tsp raw coconut oil
- 225 g/8 oz raw pecan nuts
- 2 tbsp yacon syrup
- 50 g/1¾ oz fresh stoned dates, chopped into small pieces
- pinch of pink crystal salt
- 100 g/3½ oz Buckwheaties (see page 22)

Chocolate layer
- 85 g/3 oz raw cacao butter
- 55 g/2 oz raw coconut oil
- 200 g/7 oz raw cashew nuts or raw de-hulled hemp seeds
- 200 ml/7 fl oz fresh filtered water
- 1 large avocado, halved, stoned, peeled and cubed
- 10 drops peppermint essential oil
- 125 g/4½ oz raw cacao powder, plus extra for sprinkling
- 120 g/4½ oz raw agave nectar
- 3 tbsp lucuma powder
- ¼ tsp cayenne pepper

Vanilla cream
- 100 g/1¾ oz raw coconut oil
- 150 g/5½ oz raw cashew nuts or raw de-hulled hemp seeds
- 3 tbsp xylitol crystals
- 4 drops vanilla essential oil

Icing
- 50 g/1¾ oz raw cacao butter
- 1 tbsp lucuma powder
- 1 tbsp xylitol crystals
- 3 drops peppermint essential oil

1 To make the base, if your coconut oil is rock hard, melt it gently either in a bain-marie or using a dehydrator (see pages 20–1) and then transfer it to the food processor – it doesn't have to be liquid here, so spoon it directly into the food processor if it is already soft.

2 Add the remaining ingredients for the base, except the Buckwheaties, to your food processor and process for several minutes until the date pieces have been processed as finely as possible and the mixture is stiff.

3 Add the Buckwheaties to your food processor and turn the machine on for just a couple of seconds. This will disperse the Buckwheaties throughout the other ingredients, but without them losing their crunch.

4 Transfer the mixture to the spring-form cake tin. Press firmly down into each corner of the tray and flatten using the back of a spoon or your fingers into a fairly thin, even layer – this may take a little time. Place the tin in the freezer while you make the chocolate layer.

5 Melt the cacao butter and coconut oil together gently in a bain-marie or dehydrator until runny (see pages 20–1).

6 Add the cashew nuts and water to your food processor and process until the nuts are completely broken down. Add the avocado cubes and process again until you have a creamy texture. Add the peppermint essential oil and cacao powder and process again until smooth.

7 Add the agave nectar and lucuma powder and process again, then add the melted cacao butter, coconut oil and cayenne pepper and process once more.

8 Spoon half of the mixture directly onto the base. Use a butter knife to smooth it over as flat and evenly as possible and then return the baking tray to the freezer.

9 To make the cream, melt the coconut oil as before.

10 Tip the cashew nuts into your power blender jug and blend thoroughly with the melted cacao butter and the rest of the cream ingredients until smooth. Spoon from the blender jug onto the top of the chocolate layer and take a moment to make sure that the whole cake is evenly covered. Place your cake back in the freezer while you make the icing.

11 Melt the cacao butter gently as before.

12 Add the other icing ingredients to the glass bowl and use the hand whisk in a figure-of-eight motion to whisk together until you achieve a smooth texture. Set aside for a moment.

13 To assemble, retrieve your cake from the freezer. Take your food processor containing the remaining chocolate layer mixture and spoon it on top of the vanilla cream. This is the final layer, so make it look as pretty as possible by using a butter knife to smooth it nice and flat.

14 Using a butter knife, spread the icing all over the top of the cake. Place the cake straight in the freezer on a flat surface so that the icing doesn't run and freeze for about 15 minutes.

15 Take the cake out of the freezer. Run a sharp knife around the edge and slowly release the tin. Keep refrigerated and store, covered, for up to a week.

Ice Cream Sandwich

Fun to assemble yet messy to eat, this recipe is perfect for making with children. Just bear in mind that you will need to dehydrate the biscuits and freeze the bananas the day before. I then like to lay all the components out on the table with spatulas and spoons for the kids to get stuck into. For children to really get into eating healthy foods, they need to feel involved and be given the opportunity to get excited about food. So this recipe ticks all the right boxes.

SERVES 3

EQUIPMENT
- food processor
- dehydrator with solid dehydrator sheet and mesh screen
- power blender

INGREDIENTS
Chewy chocolate biscuits
- 125 g/4½ oz raw pecan nuts
- 85 g/3 oz raw walnut halves
- pinch of pink crystal salt
- 225 g/8 oz fresh dates, stoned and halved
- 3 tbsp raw cacao powder
- 4 tbsp fresh filtered water
- 1 tbsp yacon syrup
- 20 g/¾ oz dried goji berries
- ½ tsp ground cinnamon

Ice cream
- 4 large bananas
- 50 g/1¾ oz raw agave nectar
- 4 drops vanilla essential oil

To decorate (optional)
- Pink Buckwheaties (*see* page 22)
- Buckwheaties (*see* page 22)

1 To make the biscuits, process the pecan nuts and walnuts with the salt in your food processor until roughly ground.

2 Add all the remaining ingredients to the milled nuts in the food processor and process until a dough forms.

3 Place the dough on the dehydrator sheet and roll into a large square around 5 mm/¼ inch thick. Using a sharp knife, cut the dough into individual 5-cm/2-inch square pieces. Place these on the mesh screen. Continue re-rolling the dough and cutting out squares until all the dough is used up. You should have around 14 squares in total.

4 Place the sheet in your dehydrator and dehydrate at 40.5°C/105°F for 18 hours or until firm, carefully turning the biscuits over after 4 hours. You will need 6 biscuits for the sandwiches; store the remainder in an airtight jar in the refrigerator for up to a month for a delicious and nutritious snack.

5 Meanwhile, peel and chop the bananas into 2.5-cm/1-inch pieces, then freeze for 8 hours or overnight.

6 Remove the frozen banana pieces from your freezer and place in your power blender jug. Add the agave nectar and vanilla essential oil and blend on full power, using the plunger, until thick and creamy.

7 If your children are going to assemble the sandwiches, spoon the ice cream into a mixing bowl. Otherwise, spoon it directly onto 3 of the biscuits and then top with the 3 remaining biscuits, pressing down gently.

8 If you want your children to help you, place the mixing bowl with the ice cream on the table along with a wooden chopping board and the biscuits. Give them each a spoon or spatula and watch them as they make their own masterpieces. Have a small bowlful of Pink Buckwheaties and ordinary Buckwheaties available on the table too for decoration. Eat together, straight away, for best results, and enjoy while listening to some cool music.

Raw Ice Cream Sundae

Although it might initially appear a little labour intensive to create ice cream sundaes, it will be worth it in the end when you're sitting outside in the sun with a massive serving all to yourself. This recipe works well as a dessert course for a dinner party, as you can keep the separate flavours of ice cream in bowls in the freezer, along with the frosted glasses, ready prepared until they are needed.

SERVES 4

EQUIPMENT
- **power blender**
- **bain-marie or dehydrator**

INGREDIENTS
- **2 handfuls fresh or frozen fruit for each glass, such as blueberries and raspberries**
- **2 tbsp your favourite nuts per glass, broken into pieces, such as pecan nuts**
- **4 tbsp raw agave nectar per glass**

Dark chocolate ice cream
- **250 g/9 oz raw cashew nuts**
- **70 g/2½ oz raw cacao powder**
- **250 ml/9 fl oz fresh filtered water**
- **1 tbsp raw coconut oil**
- **140 g/5 oz raw agave nectar**
- **10 drops vanilla essential oil**

Apricot and banana ice cream
- **2 tsp raw almonds**
- **4 tbsp fresh filtered water**
- **4 bananas, peeled, chopped and frozen overnight**
- **½ avocado, peeled**
- **6 ready-to-eat unsulphured dried apricots**

Cashew nut cream
- **2 tbsp raw coconut oil**
- **75 g/2¾ oz raw cashew nuts**
- **3 tbsp xylitol crystals**
- **3 drops vanilla essential oil**
- **5 tbsp fresh filtered water**
- **pinch of pink crystal salt**

1 The day before, make the Dark Chocolate Ice Cream. Process the cashew nuts in your power blender on full power, using the plunger, until they form a fine flour. Use a butter knife or chopstick to scrape the milled nuts away from the base and side of the blender jug if they have stuck.

2 Add all the remaining ingredients for the chocolate ice cream to your power blender and blend thoroughly on full speed, using the plunger, until smooth. Pour the mixture into a bowl and place in the freezer overnight.

3 To make the Apricot and Banana Ice Cream, add the ingredients to your power blender jug and blend thoroughly on full power, using the plunger, until smooth and creamy.

4 Spoon the mixture into a bowl and place in the freezer, uncovered, while you make the Cashew Nut Cream.

5 To make the cream, if your coconut oil has hardened and turned white, melt it gently in a bain-marie or dehydrator (see pages 20–1). Process the cashew nuts in your power blender on full power, using the plunger, until they form a fine powder. Use a butter knife or chopstick to scrape the milled nuts away from the base and side of the blender jug if they have stuck.

6 Add all the other ingredients to the milled nuts in the blender jug and blend on full power, using the plunger, until you have a smooth, creamy texture.

7 Take 4 large ice cream sundae glasses and place a layer of fruit in the base of each.

8 Cover the fruit with a spoonful of cream and then sprinkle with some of the broken nut pieces.

9 Take both flavours of ice cream out of the freezer and scoop each one into the glasses, making layers on top of the fruit, cream and nuts. Drizzle the agave nectar down the inside the glasses between the layers of ice cream. Eat straight away before they melt.

Milk Chocolate Fruit + Nut Clusters

These little clusters are versatile, moreish and unbelievably healthy. They're great to eat first thing in the morning covered in creamy raw almond milk (*see* page 23), or you can serve them as nibbles when you have friends over for drinks or if you have older children who can't stop foraging through the kitchen cupboards for snacks.

MAKES 60–72 PIECES

EQUIPMENT
- **bain-marie or dehydrator**
- **power blender**
- **12-hole silicone chocolate bar mould or a shallow, medium-sized BPA-free plastic container**

INGREDIENTS

Raw milk chocolate
- **50 g/1¾ oz raw cacao butter**
- **40 g/1½ oz raw hulled hemp seeds**
- **2 tbsp xylitol crystals**
- **2 tbsp raw cacao powder**
- **8 drops vanilla essential oil**
- **2 tbsp yacon syrup**
- **pinch of pink crystal salt**

Fruit and nut clusters
- **40 g/1½ oz raw walnut halves**
- **40 g/1½ oz raw cashew nuts**
- **40 g/1½ oz raw sunflower seeds**
- **40 g/1½ oz Buckwheaties (see page 22)**
- **40 g/1½ oz ready-to-eat unsulphured dried apricots, sliced into small pieces**
- **40 g/1½ oz fresh dates, stoned and sliced into small pieces**
- **20 g/¾ oz dried goji berries**
- **20 g/¾ oz raisins**

1 Melt the cacao butter gently in a bain-marie or dehydrator until runny (*see* pages 20–1).

2 Process the hemp seeds in your power blender on full power, using the plunger, until they form a fine flour. Use a butter knife or chopstick to scrape the milled seeds away from the base and side of the blender jug if they have stuck.

3 Add the melted cacao butter with all the other ingredients for the milk chocolate to the milled seeds in the blender jug and blend on full power, using your plunger, until you achieve a smooth, runny texture.

4 Pour the chocolate into a mixing bowl. Add all the remaining ingredients to the bowl and stir well with a spoon, ensuring that the raw chocolate coats the fruit and nut pieces thoroughly.

5 Spoon the mixture into the holes of the mould or a clean, dry BPA-free plastic container – 1.5 cm/⅝ inch will be deep enough. Place in the freezer for at least 15 minutes until the chocolate has set.

6 Turn your mould or container upside down onto a chopping board and pop out the fruit and nut chocolate. Using a very sharp knife, cut into 1-cm/½-inch pieces. Store in an airtight glass jar in the refrigerator for up to 3–4 weeks.

Jessica's top tip
Feel free to replace any of the fruit, nut or seed ingredients with your favourite variations, or whatever you have hidden away in your cupboards.

Cacao Crackers with Spicy Tomato + Cacao Salad Cream

Colourful and vibrant, these raw crackers include the whole raw cacao bean, which unleashes the powerful flavours of the other key ingredients, such as the heat from the chilli. They can be enjoyed dipped in the accompanying salad cream just as they are, or with a mild-flavoured topping such as chunks of avocado. The inclusion of avocado works to cool down the powerful flavours and make the spicy kick a little less intense.

MAKES ABOUT 30 SMALL CRACKERS; SERVES 4 WITH THE SALAD CREAM

EQUIPMENT

- **power blender**
- **food processor**
- **dehydrator with 2 solid dehydrator sheets and 2 mesh screens**

INGREDIENTS

Cacao crackers
- 150 g/5½ oz flax seeds
- 425 g/15 oz sweet potatoes, peeled and quartered
- 575 g/1 lb 4½ oz raw almond pulp, from roughly 2 batches of raw almond milk (*see* Raw Nut and Seed Milk, page 23)
- 3 garlic cloves, peeled
- 3 tbsp freshly squeezed lemon juice
- 140 g/5 oz peeled red onion
- 1 tsp chilli powder
- ½ tsp black peppercorns
- 1 tsp turmeric
- 1 tsp pink crystal salt
- 250 ml/9 fl oz fresh filtered water
- 35 g/1¼ oz raw cacao beans
- 40 g/1½ oz fresh dates, stoned
- 85 g/3 oz peeled beetroot

Salad cream
- 300 g/10½ oz fresh ripe tomatoes
- 1 large garlic clove, peeled
- 1 tbsp raw coconut oil
- 40 g/1½ oz raw cashew nuts
- 50 ml/2 fl oz freshly squeezed lemon juice
- 20 g/¾ oz raw cacao nibs
- 6 fresh dates, stoned
- ½ tsp hot chilli powder
- pinch of pink crystal salt

1 For the crackers, process the flax seeds in your power blender on full power, using the plunger, until they form a fine flour.

2 Transfer the milled seeds to your food processor, add the almond pulp and process until thoroughly mixed. Spoon into a large mixing bowl.

3 Add all the remaining ingredients for the crackers to your power blender jug and process on full power, using the plunger, until smooth. Pour into the mixing bowl and stir all the ingredients together.

4 Spread the mixture evenly onto the solid dehydrator sheets to a depth of 5 mm/¼ inch, taking the mixture up to 2 cm/¾ inch away from the edges of the sheets. Using a butter knife, score lines down and cross the mixture to mark into 5-cm/2-inch squares.

5 Place the sheets in the dehydrator and dehydrate for 9 hours at 40.5°C/105°F. Flip onto the mesh screens and peel the sheets away. Place the mesh screens in the dehydrator and dehydrate the biscuits for a further 12 hours or until solid and crispy. They can be stored in an airtight glass jar in a cool, dry place for up to a month.

6 To make the salad cream, add all the ingredients to your washed and dried power blender jug and blend on full power, using the plunger, until smooth and creamy. Serve with the cacao crackers. The salad cream will keep in an airtight glass jar in the refrigerator for up to 24 hours, although fresh is always best.

Index

agave nectar 16
Almond Butter Truffles 50
antioxidants 7, 10, 12

Banana Split 84
Beetroot & Mint Choc Chip
  Sorbet 68
Birthday Cake 86–7
Buckwheaties 19, 22

Cacao & Coconut Water Shake 26
Cacao Crackers with Spicy Tomato &
  Cacao Salad Cream 94
Cacao Maca Boost 28
caffeine 13
Chocolate Goji Finger Biscuits 59
Choctail Mocktail 28
Chronic Fatigue Syndrome (CFS) 6–7
Cinnamon-flavoured Raw Chocolate
  Bars 45
Crêpes 82

diabetics 15, 18
Double-dunked Raw Chocolate
  Truffles 42
dried goji berries 16

equipment 20–1
essential fats 13
essential oils 16, 18

flax seeds 17
Fresh Cherry & Chocolate Truffles 38

Ginger Caramels 48
Guarana & Goji Nutty Loaf 70
guarana powder 17

health benefits 7, 10, 12–13
hemp seeds 17

Ice Cream Sandwich 89

Little Leo's Pudding 73
Love Macaroons 64
lucuma powder 15

maca powder 17
magnesium 12
Milk Chocolate Fruit & Nut
  Clusters 93
Myalgic Encephalomyelitis (ME) 6-7

Neapolitan Ice Cream 66–7

Peppermint Creams 46
Pink Buckwheaties 19, 22
pink crystal salt 17
pregnancy 17, 18
purple corn extract powder 17

raw cacao beans 10, 11, 15
raw cacao butter 11, 14
Raw Cacao Fudge 34
raw cacao nibs 14
raw cacao paste 14
raw cacao powder 10, 11, 14
Raw Chocochino 26
Raw Chocolate & Banana
  Smoothie 30
Raw Chocolate Brownies 54–5
Raw Chocolate Cheesecake 52
Raw Chocolate Gingerbread
  People 62
Raw Chocolate Jellies 80
Raw Chocolate-coated Brazils 33

raw coconut oil 17
Raw Hemp & Chocolate Spread 79
Raw Ice Cream Sundae 90
raw nut & seed butters 16, 23
raw nut & seed flour 19, 23
raw nut & seed milk 19, 23
Rich Raw Chocolate & Vanilla
  Torte 56–7

sulphur 12
Summer Sorbet 68

Tangy Lemon Chocolates 36
theobromine 13, 18
Tingly Raw Chocolate Body Paint 76

vanilla pods 17, 18
vegan diet 7, 18

White & Dark Orange Creams 40
White Chocolate & Raisin Snaps 60
White Raw Choc Chip Pudding 74
Winter Warming Drinking
  Chocolate 30

xylitol crystals 15

yacon syrup 15

Acknowledgements

The publisher would like to thank Vitamix and UK Juicers for the loan of equipment for the photoshoot; Raw Gaia and Total Raw Food for supplying ingredients and Aloka, Dirty Harry, Mange Tout, Pulse Organics and the Taj Mahal in Brighton, UK, for allowing us to photograph at their premises.